# CAKES

*by*
*Jean Paré*

**companyscoming.com**
visit our web-site

# Dedication

*If I knew you were coming . . . I'd have baked a cake!*

**Cover Photo**

Chocolate Mocha Cake page 59
with Coffee Icing page 150

# CAKES

Ninth Printing July 2003

**Canadian Cataloguing in Publication Data**

Paré, Jean
Company's Coming cakes

Includes index.
ISBN 0-9693322-3-8

1. Cake. I. Title. II. Title: Cakes.

TX771.P37 1990          641.8'653    C90-013237-X


Published and Distributed by
Company's Coming Publishing Limited
2311–96 Street
Edmonton, Alberta, Canada
T6N 1G3


**Published Simultaneously in
Canada and the United States of America**

**Printed In Canada**

# Company's Coming Cookbook Series

Quick & easy recipes, everyday ingredients!

### Original Series

- Softcover, 160 pages
- 6" x 9" (15 cm x 23 cm) format
- Lay-flat binding
- Full colour photos
- Nutrition information

### Greatest Hits Series

- Softcover, 106 & 124 pages
- 8" x 9 9/16" (20 cm x 24 cm) format
- Paperback binding
- Full colour photos
- Nutrition information

### Lifestyle Series

- Softcover, 160 pages
- 8" x 10" (20 cm x 25 cm) format
- Paperback & spiral binding
- Full colour photos
- Nutrition information

### Special Occasion Series

- Hardcover & softcover, 192 pages
- 8 1/2" x 11" (22 cm x 28 cm) format
- Durable sewn binding
- Full colour throughout
- Nutrition information

See page 157
for a complete listing
of **all** cookbooks
or visit
companyscoming.com

# table of Contents

# the Jean Paré story

Jean Paré grew up understanding that the combination of family, friends and home cooking is the essence of a good life. From her mother she learned to appreciate good cooking, while her father praised even her earliest attempts. When she left home she took with her many acquired family recipes, her love of cooking and her intriguing desire to read recipe books like novels!

In 1963, when her four children had all reached school age, Jean volunteered to cater to the 50th anniversary of the Vermilion School of Agriculture, now Lakeland College. Working out of her home, Jean prepared a dinner for over 1000 people which launched a flourishing catering operation that continued for over eighteen years. During that time she was provided with countless opportunities to test new ideas with immediate feedback—resulting in empty plates and contented customers! Whether preparing cocktail sandwiches for a house party or serving a hot meal for 1500 people, Jean Paré earned a reputation for good food, courteous service and reasonable prices.

"Why don't you write a cookbook?" Time and again, as requests for her recipes mounted, Jean was asked that question. Jean's response was to team up with her son, Grant Lovig, in the fall of 1980 to form Company's Coming Publishing Limited. April 14, 1981, marked the debut of "150 DELICIOUS SQUARES", the first Company's Coming cookbook in what soon would become Canada's most popular cookbook series.

Jean Paré's operation has grown steadily from the early days of working out of a spare bedroom in her home. Full-time staff includes marketing personnel located in major cities across Canada. Home Office is based in Edmonton, Alberta in a modern building constructed specially for the company.

Today the company distributes throughout Canada and the United States in addition to numerous overseas markets, all under the guidance of Jean's daughter, Gail Lovig. Best-sellers many times over in English, Company's Coming cookbooks have also been published in French and Spanish. Familiar and trusted in home kitchens around the world, Company's Coming cookbooks are offered in a variety of formats, including the original softcover series.

Jean Paré's approach to cooking has always called for quick and easy recipes using everyday ingredients. Even when travelling, she is constantly on the lookout for new ideas to share with her readers. At home, she can usually be found researching and writing recipes, or working in the company's test kitchen. Jean continues to gain new supporters by adhering to what she calls "the golden rule of cooking": never share a recipe you wouldn't use yourself. It's an approach that works—*millions of times over!*

# Foreword

Cake is an irresistible treat—morning, noon or night. The temptation begins with the heavenly aroma of homemade cake baking in the oven. Awaken your tastebuds with early morning coffee and Mocha Cake or Chocolate Oatmeal Cake. Surprise the young ones with Chip and Date Cake in their lunch boxes. Treat yourself and your friends to Sultana Cake at afternoon tea or the classic Lady Baltimore as the finale to a glorious meal.

When making a cake, it is essential to preheat your oven to the correct temperature. Baking times given in this book are approximate due to slight variations in the heat of ovens. A thermometer for inside your oven is a good investment. To prevent cakes from falling, do not open the oven door until three-quarters of baking time has elapsed. Check to see if your cake is cooked by inserting a wooden pick in the center. If it comes out clean and dry, the cake is done. Another way to tell is to watch for the cake to begin shrinking from the sides of the pan.

You can prepare ahead of time by greasing your cake pans. Only the bottoms (not sides) of the pans need to be greased in most cases. When a recipe calls for an ungreased pan that is to be inverted to cool, the pan must be completely grease-free. For a larger tube cake, consider using an angel food tube pan as it has a flat bottom and therefore holds more batter than a bundt tube pan.

Ingredients are best mixed at room temperature. If separating eggs, do so when they are cold and let them come to room temperature. Never beat egg whites in plastic bowls as the grease in the plastic will prevent them from becoming light and fluffy. Also, watch that no bit of egg yolk is in the whites before beating. For best results use large eggs in cake recipes.

Over-mixing cake batter may result in failure. Most attention should be given to the creaming of the butter (or margarine or shortening), sugar and eggs. Once thoroughly mixed, incorporate the remaining ingredients and mix with a light hand until evenly blended. Sift dry ingredients such as icing (confectioner's) sugar or cocoa before adding. If a recipe calls for cake flour and you do not have any on hand, simply substitute all-purpose flour but use two tablespoons (30 mL) less per cup (250 mL) of flour required.

All cakes may be frozen. They keep longer if frozen uniced and unfilled. If you choose to ice the cake, freeze it before wrapping. Heavily fruited cakes keep well in a cool place but lightly fruited cakes should be frozen. Do not store fruitcake in foil as the acid in the fruit will corrode the foil.

This book contains cakes of every variety plus a vast assortment of icings, fillings and frostings. There are small cakes, large cakes and in-between cakes. When company's coming, whip up a one-bowl cake, take a cake from the freezer or create a sensational multi-layered cake. No matter how you slice it, there is a cake for everyone and any occasion.

Jean Paré.

# OLD HERMIT CAKE

*This is a huge cake. It is so good you will think it is full of hermit cookies. Recipe is over one hundred years old. "Use butter" it warns.*

| | | |
|---|---|---|
| Butter (not margarine), softened | 2 cups | 450 mL |
| Brown sugar, packed | 3 cups | 700 mL |
| Eggs | 6 | 6 |
| Juice from lemon | 1 | 1 |
| Vanilla | 4 tsp. | 20 mL |
| All-purpose flour | 4 1/2 cups | 1 L |
| Baking powder | 4 tsp. | 20 mL |
| Cinnamon | 2 tsp. | 10 mL |
| Salt | 1/4 tsp. | 1 mL |
| Chopped dates | 3 cups | 700 mL |
| Chopped walnuts | 3 cups | 700 mL |

Preheat oven to 275°F (140°C). Cream butter and sugar together well. Beat in eggs 1 at a time. Mix in lemon juice and vanilla.

Add remaining ingredients. Stir well. Turn into greased and floured 10 inch (25 cm) angel food tube pan. Bake in oven for about 2 1/2 to 3 hours until an inserted wooden pick comes out clean.

# DATE CAKE

*Try this in a multitude of different ways. Sprinkle with a crumb mixture before baking, spread with a topping after baking or cool and ice with an orange or a peanut butter icing. Even served with whipped cream it's good. Moist.*

| | | |
|---|---|---|
| Chopped dates | 1 cup | 250 mL |
| Boiling water | 1 cup | 250 mL |
| Butter or margarine, softened | 1/2 cup | 125 mL |
| Granulated sugar | 1 cup | 250 mL |
| Egg | 1 | 1 |
| Vanilla | 1 tsp. | 5 mL |
| All-purpose flour | 1 1/2 cups | 375 mL |
| Baking soda | 1 tsp. | 5 mL |
| Salt | 1/4 tsp. | 1 mL |
| Chopped walnuts | 1/2 cup | 125 mL |

*(continued on next page)*

Preheat oven to 350°F (180°C). Put dates into bowl. Add boiling water. Let stand until cool.

Cream butter and sugar together. Beat in egg and vanilla.

Combine flour, baking soda and salt. Add to butter mixture in 3 parts alternately with cooled date-water mixture in 2 parts, beginning and ending with flour mixture.

Stir in walnuts. Spread in greased 9 × 9 inch (22 × 22 cm) pan. Cover with Nutty Crumb Topping if using. Bake in oven for 30 to 35 minutes until an inserted wooden pick comes out clean.

### NUTTY CRUMB TOPPING

| | | |
|---|---|---|
| Butter or margarine | 2 tbsp. | 30 mL |
| All-purpose flour | 1/4 cup | 60 mL |
| Granulated sugar | 1/4 cup | 60 mL |
| Chopped nuts | 1/2 cup | 125 mL |

Mix all 4 ingredients together until crumbly. Sprinkle over cake before baking.

### QUICK BOILED TOPPING

| | | |
|---|---|---|
| Butter or margarine | 3 tbsp. | 50 mL |
| Cream | 6 tbsp. | 100 mL |
| Brown sugar, packed | 6 tbsp. | 100 mL |
| Coconut | 6 tbsp. | 100 mL |

Combine all 4 ingredients in small saucepan over medium heat. Bring to a boil. Stir often. Boil for 3 minutes. Spread over hot baked cake.

*No wonder fish is such good brain food. They always travel in schools.*

# BANANA CAKE

*Good keeping qualities to this moist cake.*

| | | |
|---|---|---|
| Butter or margarine, softened | 1/2 cup | 125 mL |
| Granulated sugar | 1 1/2 cups | 350 mL |
| Eggs | 2 | 2 |
| Vanilla | 1 tsp. | 5 mL |
| Mashed banana | 1 cup | 225 mL |
| Buttermilk or sour milk | 1/3 cup | 75 mL |
| All-purpose flour | 2 cups | 450 mL |
| Baking powder | 1 tsp. | 5 mL |
| Baking soda | 1 tsp. | 5 mL |
| Salt | 1/2 tsp. | 2 mL |

Preheat oven to 350°F (180°C). Cream butter and sugar together. Beat in eggs 1 at a time. Add vanilla.

Mix banana with buttermilk.

Sift flour, baking powder, baking soda and salt together. Add to butter mixture in 3 parts alternately with banana mixture in 2 parts, beginning and ending with flour. Spread in 2 greased round 8 inch (20 cm) layer pans. Bake in oven for 25 to 35 minutes or until an inserted wooden pick comes out clean. Cool. Fill and frost with Butter Icing, page 150 or Peanut Butter Icing, page 141.

# LEMON CAKE

*This will go fast. Great flavor with a great glaze. No icing needed.*

| | | |
|---|---|---|
| Butter or margarine, softened | 3/4 cup | 175 mL |
| Brown sugar, packed | 1 cup | 225 mL |
| Granulated sugar | 1/4 cup | 60 mL |
| Eggs | 2 | 2 |
| All-purpose flour | 2 cups | 450 mL |
| Baking powder | 1 tsp. | 5 mL |
| Baking soda | 1 tsp. | 5 mL |
| Salt | 1/4 tsp. | 1 mL |
| Sour milk, see Note | 1 cup | 225 mL |
| Grated rind of lemon | 1 | 1 |
| Chopped dates | 1 cup | 250 mL |

*(continued on next page)*

Preheat oven to 350°F (180°C). Cream butter and sugars together. Beat in eggs 1 at a time.

Stir next 4 dry ingredients in small bowl.

Add flour mixture to butter mixture in 3 parts alternately with sour milk in 2 parts, beginning and ending with flour.

Stir in lemon rind and dates. Mix until blended. Spread in greased 9 × 13 inch (22 × 33 cm) pan. Bake in oven for about 40 minutes until an inserted wooden pick comes out clean.

**Topping:** Heat 1¹/₂ tbsp. (25 mL) lemon juice and ¹/₂ cup (125 mL) brown sugar. Stir to dissolve. Spoon over hot cake.

**Note:** To make sour milk, add milk to 1 tbsp. (15 mL) vinegar in measuring cup. Stir.

# APPLESAUCE CAKE

*A no-fuss way to get apples into a cake. Spicy good with a slight hint of cloves. Darkish color.*

| | | |
|---|---|---|
| Butter or margarine, softened | ¹/₂ cup | 125 mL |
| Granulated sugar | ³/₄ cup | 175 mL |
| Egg | 1 | 1 |
| All-purpose flour | 1¹/₂ cups | 375 mL |
| Salt | 1 tsp. | 5 mL |
| Baking soda | 1 tsp. | 5 mL |
| Cinnamon | 1 tsp. | 5 mL |
| Cloves | ¹/₄ tsp. | 1 mL |
| Chopped walnuts | 1 cup | 250 mL |
| Chopped raisins | 1 cup | 250 mL |
| Sweetened applesauce or puréed baby food apricots | 1 cup | 250 mL |

Preheat oven to 350°F (180°C). Cream butter and sugar together in mixing bowl. Beat in egg.

Combine next 7 ingredients in separate bowl.

Heat applesauce to simmering. Add to butter mixture 2 parts alternately with dry mixture in 3 parts, beginning and ending with dry mixture. Spread in greased 8 × 8 inch (20 × 20 cm) pan. Bake in oven for about 40 to 45 minutes or until an inserted wooden pick comes out clean.

# APPLE BRAN CAKE

*Fresh apples and all-bran cereal combine to make this great taste.*

| | | |
|---|---|---|
| Butter or margarine, softened | 1/2 cup | 125 mL |
| Granulated sugar | 1 cup | 250 mL |
| Eggs | 2 | 2 |
| All-purpose flour | 1 1/2 cups | 375 mL |
| Baking soda | 2 tsp. | 10 mL |
| Cinnamon | 1 1/2 tsp. | 7 mL |
| Nutmeg | 1/2 tsp. | 2 mL |
| Salt | 1/2 tsp. | 2 mL |
| All-bran cereal | 1 cup | 250 mL |
| Peeled, diced apple | 4 cups | 900 mL |

Preheat oven to 350°F (180°C). Cream butter and sugar together well. Beat in eggs 1 at a time.

Add remaining ingredients. Stir until mixed together well. Turn into greased 9 × 9 inch (22 × 22 cm) pan. Bake in oven until an inserted wooden pick comes out clean, about 45 minutes. Cool.

# APPLE SURPRISE CAKE

*The surprise ingredient is Worcestershire sauce. You will have to try it to see how good it is. The best!*

| | | |
|---|---|---|
| Eggs | 2 | 2 |
| Granulated sugar | 2 cups | 450 mL |
| Cooking oil | 1 cup | 225 mL |
| Worcestershire sauce | 1 tbsp. | 15 mL |
| All-purpose flour | 3 cups | 700 mL |
| Baking soda | 2 tsp. | 10 mL |
| Cinnamon | 2 tsp. | 10 mL |
| Nutmeg | 1/2 tsp. | 2 mL |
| Cloves | 1/4 tsp. | 1 mL |
| Salt | 1 tsp. | 5 mL |
| Diced, unpeeled apple | 4 cups | 900 mL |
| Chopped walnuts | 1 cup | 250 mL |
| Chopped raisins | 1 cup | 250 mL |

*(continued on next page)*

Preheat oven to 325°F (160°C). Beat eggs until frothy. Beat in sugar, cooking oil and Worcestershire sauce.

Combine next 6 ingredients. Add to wet ingredients. Stir.

Add apple, walnuts and raisins. Stir. Batter will be stiff. Turn into greased and floured 12 cup (2.7 L) bundt pan. Bake in oven until an inserted wooden pick comes out clean, about 1¹/₄ hours. Let stand 20 minutes. Turn out onto plate.

# BANANA CHOCOLATE CAKE

*Surprise! You will think you are biting into a chocolate cake and then you taste banana. For an extra treat, frost with a peanut butter icing.*

| | | |
|---|---|---|
| **Butter or margarine, softened** | ³/₄ cup | 175 mL |
| **Granulated sugar** | 1³/₄ cups | 400 mL |
| **Eggs** | 2 | 2 |
| **Mashed banana** | 1¹/₄ cups | 275 mL |
| **Vanilla** | 1 tsp. | 5 mL |
| **All-purpose flour** | 2 cups | 450 mL |
| **Cocoa** | ³/₄ cup | 175 mL |
| **Baking powder** | 1¹/₂ tsp. | 7 mL |
| **Baking soda** | 1 tsp. | 5 mL |
| **Salt** | ³/₄ tsp. | 4 mL |
| **Sour milk, see Note** | ³/₄ cup | 175 mL |

Preheat oven to 350°F (180°C). Cream butter with sugar and 1 egg together very well. Beat in second egg. Mix in banana and vanilla.

Mix flour, cocoa, baking powder, baking soda and salt together in small bowl.

Add flour mixture to butter mixture in 3 parts alternately with sour milk in 2 parts, beginning and ending with flour. Spread in 2 greased round 8 or 9 inch (20 or 22 cm) layer pans. Bake in oven until an inserted wooden pick comes out clean, about 40 minutes. Frost with Peanut Butter Icing, page 141 or Chocolate Cheese Icing, page 145.

**Note:** To make sour milk, add milk to 1 tbsp. (15 mL) vinegar in measuring cup. Stir.

# MATRIMONIAL CAKE

*This is one of those time honored cakes. A real treat when served hot with ice cream.*

| | | |
|---|---|---|
| Chopped dates | 1²/₃ cups | 400 mL |
| Water | 1 cup | 250 mL |
| Granulated sugar | ¹/₂ cup | 125 mL |
| Lemon juice | 1 tsp. | 5 mL |
| Vanilla | 1 tsp. | 5 mL |
| All-purpose flour | 1¹/₂ cups | 375 mL |
| Oatmeal | 1¹/₂ cups | 375 mL |
| Brown sugar, packed | 1 cup | 250 mL |
| Baking soda | 1 tsp. | 5 mL |
| Salt | ¹/₂ tsp. | 2 mL |
| Butter or margarine, softened | 1 cup | 250 mL |

Preheat oven to 350°F (180°C). Combine first 5 ingredients in medium saucepan. Bring to a gentle simmer. Cook until smooth and of spreading consistency.

Meanwhile measure next 6 ingredients into large bowl. Cut in butter until mixture is crumbly. Pack ²/₃ of crumb mixture into greased 9 × 9 inch (22 × 22 cm) pan. Spread hot date mixture over top. Cover with remaining crumbs. Press lightly. Bake in oven for 30 to 35 minutes until browned.

Pictured on page 125.

# APPLE PINE CAKE

*A delicious combination. It has a faint rosy tint. A good moist cake.*

| | | |
|---|---|---|
| Eggs | 3 | 3 |
| Cooking oil | ¹/₂ cup | 125 mL |
| Crushed pineapple, drained | 14 oz. | 398 mL |
| Granulated sugar | 1¹/₂ cups | 350 mL |
| Peeled, diced apples | 3 cups | 700 mL |
| Vanilla | 1 tsp. | 5 mL |
| Almond flavoring | 1 tsp. | 5 mL |

*(continued on next page)*

| All-purpose flour | 2¼ cups | 500 mL |
|---|---|---|
| Baking soda | 2 tsp. | 10 mL |
| Cinnamon | 2 tsp. | 10 mL |
| Nutmeg | ¼ tsp. | 1 mL |
| Salt | 1 tsp. | 5 mL |
| Chopped walnuts | 1 cup | 250 mL |
| Chopped raisins | ½ cup | 125 mL |

Preheat oven to 350°F (180°C). Beat eggs in mixing bowl until frothy.

Add next 6 ingredients. Mix with a spoon.

Mix remaining ingredients together in small bowl. Add. Stir to mix well. Batter will be stiff. Pour into greased 9 × 13 inch (22 × 33 cm) pan. Bake in oven for about 45 minutes until an inserted wooden pick comes out clean.

# DATE OATMEAL CAKE

*This ancient recipe makes a firm tasty cake. It can be glazed or even sliced and buttered if you'd rather.*

| Butter or margarine, softened | ¼ cup | 60 mL |
|---|---|---|
| Granulated sugar | ¾ cup | 175 mL |
| Egg | 1 | 1 |
| Salt | ½ tsp. | 2 mL |
| Buttermilk | 1 cup | 250 mL |
| Baking soda | 1 tsp. | 5 mL |
| Oatmeal | ¾ cup | 175 mL |
| Chopped dates | 1 cup | 250 mL |
| Chopped nuts, your choice | 1 cup | 250 mL |
| All-purpose flour | 1½ cups | 375 mL |
| Baking powder | 1 tsp. | 5 mL |

Preheat oven to 350°F (180°C). Measure butter, sugar, egg and salt into mixing bowl. Cream together until fluffy. Slowly mix in buttermilk and baking soda.

Stir in oatmeal, dates and nuts.

Stir flour and baking powder together. Stir into batter. Spread in greased 8 × 8 inch (20 × 20 cm) pan. Bake in oven for 45 minutes or until an inserted wooden pick comes out clean. Cool. Pour Brown Sugar Glaze, page 146, over top.

# HUMMINGBIRD CAKE

*Crushed pineapple, diced banana and pecans all help to make this moist and nutty. Good size.*

| | | |
|---|---|---|
| All-purpose flour | 3 cups | 750 mL |
| Granulated sugar | 2 cups | 500 mL |
| Baking soda | 1 tsp. | 5 mL |
| Salt | $1/2$ tsp. | 2 mL |
| Cinnamon | 1 tsp. | 5 mL |
| Cooking oil | $1^1/_4$ cups | 300 mL |
| Eggs | 3 | 3 |
| Vanilla | 1 tsp. | 5 mL |
| Crushed pineapple with juice | 1 cup | 250 mL |
| Diced banana | 2 cups | 500 mL |
| Chopped pecans or walnuts | 1 cup | 250 mL |

Preheat oven to 350°F (180°C). Measure first 8 ingredients into mixing bowl. Beat until smooth.

Add pineapple with juice, banana and pecans. Stir with a spoon to mix in. Pour into greased and floured 12 cup (2.7 L) bundt pan. Bake in oven for about 1 hour and 10 minutes. Turn out onto rack or plate after cooling for 20 minutes. Cool and ice with Cream Cheese Icing, page 145.

1. Cone Cupcakes page 116 with Peanut Butter Icing page 141
2. Cone Cupcakes page 116 with Green Butter Icing page 150
3. Cone Cupcakes page 116 with Lemon Icing page 150
4. Turtle Cake page 133
5. Confetti Angel Food page 27 with Pink Butter Icing page 150
6. Popcorn Cake page 100

*Scrumptious! Not too much height to this. Just right to get some topping with every bite.*

| | | |
|---|---|---|
| Boiling water | 1 cup | 250 mL |
| Chopped dates | 1 cup | 250 mL |
| Butter or margarine, softened | 1/4 cup | 60 mL |
| Granulated sugar | 1 cup | 250 mL |
| Egg | 1 | 1 |
| Vanilla | 1 tsp. | 5 mL |
| All-purpose flour | 1 1/2 cups | 375 mL |
| Baking soda | 1 tsp. | 5 mL |
| Baking powder | 1 tsp. | 5 mL |
| Salt | 1/2 tsp. | 2 mL |
| Chopped walnuts | 1/2 cup | 125 mL |
| **COCONUT TOPPING** | | |
| Coconut | 1 cup | 250 mL |
| Brown sugar, packed | 2/3 cup | 150 mL |
| Butter or margarine | 6 tbsp. | 100 mL |
| Cream or milk | 1/4 cup | 60 mL |

Preheat oven to 350°F (180°C). Pour boiling water over dates in bowl. Let stand until cool.

Cream butter and sugar together in mixing bowl. Beat in egg and vanilla.

Measure remaining 5 ingredients into small bowl. Stir to mix. Add to butter mixture in 3 parts alternately with date mixture in 2 parts, beginning and ending with dry mixture. Spread in greased 9 × 13 inch (22 × 33 cm) pan. Bake in oven for 30 to 40 minutes until an inserted wooden pick comes out clean. Proceed with topping that follows.

**Coconut Topping:** Mix all 4 ingredients in small saucepan over medium heat. Boil for 3 minutes. Spread over warm cake. Brown under broiler.

Pictured on page 125.

Paré Pointer

*In the fall the best car to drive is an autumn-mobile.*

# DATE ORANGE CAKE

*A medium dark cake which is moist. A good combination.*

| | | |
|---|---|---|
| Butter or margarine, softened | 1/2 cup | 125 mL |
| Brown sugar, packed | 1 1/2 cups | 375 mL |
| Eggs | 2 | 2 |
| Grated orange rind | 2 tbsp. | 30 mL |
| Chopped dates | 1 cup | 250 mL |
| Chopped pecans or walnuts | 1 cup | 250 mL |
| All-purpose flour | 2 3/4 cups | 675 mL |
| Baking soda | 1 tsp. | 5 mL |
| Baking powder | 1 tsp. | 5 mL |
| Salt | 1/2 tsp. | 2 mL |
| Buttermilk or sour milk | 1 2/3 cups | 400 mL |

Preheat oven to 350°F (180°C). Cream butter and sugar well. Beat in eggs 1 at a time. Add orange rind, dates and pecans. Stir.

Sift flour, baking soda, baking powder and salt into bowl.

Add flour mixture to butter mixture in 3 parts alternately with buttermilk in 2 parts, beginning and ending with flour. Turn into greased and floured 10 inch (25 cm) angel food tube pan. Bake in oven for about 1 hour until an inserted wooden pick comes out clean. Pour glaze over top of hot cake.

**GLAZE:** Heat to dissolve 1/4 cup (60 mL) each of granulated sugar and orange juice and 1/4 tsp. (1 mL) lemon juice. Spoon over cake.

**CRUSTY GLAZE:** Mix glaze ingredients but do not heat. Just stir together and spoon over hot cake.

# EGG YOLK SPONGE

*A good recipe to use leftover egg yolks.*

| | | |
|---|---|---|
| Egg yolks, room temperature | 4 | 4 |
| Warm water | 2 tbsp. | 30 mL |
| Granulated sugar | 1/2 cup | 125 mL |
| All-purpose flour | 1/2 cup | 125 mL |
| Cream of tartar | 1/2 tsp. | 2 mL |
| Hot milk | 2 tbsp. | 30 mL |
| Baking soda | 1/2 tsp. | 2 mL |

*(continued on next page)*

Preheat oven to 350°F (180°C). In mixing bowl beat egg yolks and warm water together until thick and lemon colored. Add sugar gradually, beating until dissolved.

Add flour and cream of tartar. Fold in.

Mix milk with baking soda. Fold into batter. Spread in greased 8 × 8 inch (20 × 20 cm) pan. Bake in oven for 25 to 30 minutes until an inserted wooden pick comes out clean. Cool. Ice with Butter Icing, page 150.

# BANANA OAT CAKE

*A moist cake, good flavored in itself but with the chocolate chips it is special.*

| | | |
|---|---|---|
| Butter or margarine, softened | 1 cup | 225 mL |
| Granulated sugar | 1 cup | 225 mL |
| Eggs | 2 | 2 |
| Mashed banana | 1 cup | 225 mL |
| Sour milk, see Note | 1/2 cup | 125 mL |
| Vanilla | 1 tsp. | 5 mL |
| All-purpose flour | 2 cups | 450 mL |
| Quick cooking rolled oats | 1 cup | 225 mL |
| Baking soda | 1 tsp. | 5 mL |
| Baking powder | 1 tsp. | 5 mL |
| Salt | 1/2 tsp. | 2 mL |
| Semisweet chocolate chips | 1 cup | 250 mL |

Preheat oven to 350°F (180°C). Cream butter and sugar together. Beat in eggs 1 at a time.

Add banana, sour milk and vanilla. Mix.

Measure in flour, rolled oats, baking soda, baking powder, salt and chocolate chips. Mix together well with spoon. Turn into greased 9 × 13 inch (22 × 33 cm) pan. Bake in oven for 30 to 35 minutes until an inserted wooden pick comes out clean. Cool.

**Note:** To make sour milk, add milk to 1 tbsp. (15 mL) vinegar in measuring cup. Stir.

# CHERRY CHIFFON CAKE

*A light texture with the prettiest pink color. Bits of cherries add to the color. Double the recipe to make the usual chiffon cake size.*

| | | |
|---|---|---|
| All-purpose flour | 1 cup | 250 mL |
| Granulated sugar | 3/4 cup | 175 mL |
| Baking powder | 1 1/2 tsp. | 7 mL |
| Salt | 1/2 tsp. | 2 mL |
| Cooking oil | 1/4 cup | 60 mL |
| Egg yolks, room temperature | 2 | 2 |
| Maraschino cherry syrup | 1/4 cup | 60 mL |
| Water | 2 tbsp. | 30 mL |
| Vanilla | 1/2 tsp. | 2 mL |
| Almond flavoring | 1 tsp. | 5 mL |
| Egg whites, room temperature | 1/2 cup | 125 mL |
| Cream of tartar | 1/4 tsp. | 1 mL |
| Finely chopped maraschino cherries | 1/2 cup | 125 mL |

Preheat oven to 325°F (160°C). Wash angel food tube pan in hot soapy water to ensure it is totally grease-free. Sift flour, sugar, baking powder and salt into bowl. Make a well in center.

Into well, put cooking oil, egg yolks, cherry syrup, water, vanilla and almond flavoring. Set aside. Don't beat yet.

Beat egg whites and cream of tartar until very stiff. Set aside.

Using same beaters, beat egg yolk-flour mixture until smooth. Fold 1/4 at a time gently into egg whites.

Add cherries. Fold in. Pour into ungreased 10 inch (25 cm) angel food tube pan. Bake in oven for about 45 to 50 minutes until an inserted wooden pick comes out clean. Invert pan until cake has cooled. Ice with Cherry Icing, page 150. Drizzle with melted chocolate around outside edge.

Pictured without icing on page 53.

*He is in such poor shape he gets exhausted by wrestling with his conscience.*

*This makes a splendid, large cake.*

| | | |
|---|---|---|
| Milk | ³/₄ cup | 175 mL |
| Poppy seeds | ¹/₂ cup | 125 mL |
| Sifted cake flour | 2 cups | 450 mL |
| Granulated sugar | 1¹/₂ cups | 350 mL |
| Baking powder | 1 tbsp. | 15 mL |
| Salt | 1 tsp. | 5 mL |
| Cooking oil | ¹/₂ cup | 125 mL |
| Egg yolks, room temperature | 7 | 7 |
| Vanilla | 2 tsp. | 10 mL |
| Lemon flavoring | 1 tsp. | 5 mL |
| Egg whites, room temperature | 7 | 7 |
| Cream of tartar | ¹/₂ tsp. | 2 mL |

Preheat oven to 325°F (160°C). Wash angel food tube pan in hot soapy water to ensure it is totally grease-free. Combine milk and poppy seeds in small bowl. Let stand 2 hours.

Sift flour, sugar, baking powder and salt into medium mixing bowl. Make a well in center.

Add next 4 ingredients to well in order given. Add poppy seed mixture to well. Set aside. Don't beat yet.

In large mixing bowl beat egg whites and cream of tartar until very stiff.

Using same beaters beat egg yolk-flour mixture until smooth and light. Pour ¹/₄ at a time over beaten egg whites folding in with rubber spatula until all traces of flour disappear. Do not stir. Pour into ungreased 10 inch (25 cm) angel food tube pan. Bake in oven for 55 minutes. Increase heat to 350°F (180°C) and bake 10 to 15 minutes more until an inserted wooden pick comes out clean. Invert pan to cool. Ice with Vanilla Glaze, page 146, Caramel Icing, page 138 or Seafoam Frosting, page 147.

Pictured with Caramel Icing on page 125.

*Pare Pointer*

*Save for a rainy day. Become an old soak.*

# JELLY ROLL

*Pretty as a picture. A great roll that you should try.*

| | | |
|---|---|---|
| Eggs, room temperature | 4 | 4 |
| Granulated sugar | 3/4 cup | 175 mL |
| Vanilla | 1 tsp. | 5 mL |
| Sifted cake flour | 7/8 cup | 200 mL |
| Baking powder | 1 tsp. | 5 mL |
| Salt | 1/4 tsp. | 1 mL |

Icing (confectioner's) sugar

Raspberry jam or other filling

Raspberry Sauce (optional)

First prepare 10 × 15 inch (25 × 38 cm) jelly roll pan. Grease well. Line bottom with waxed paper. Preheat oven to 350°F (180°C).

Beat eggs in small mixing bowl until frothy. Beating at high speed, slowly sprinkle in granulated sugar. Add vanilla. Continue beating until mixture becomes quite thick. This will take about five minutes at least. Transfer contents to large mixing bowl for best folding-in results.

Sift cake flour once then measure required amount. Add baking powder and salt to flour. Stir lightly. Fold into egg mixture one third at a time until all is moistened. Spread into prepared jelly roll pan. Bake in oven for about 20 minutes.

Turn out immediately onto clean tea towel covered heavily with sifted icing sugar. Carefully remove waxed paper. Trim crisp edges if any as they will crack when rolled.

Spread with jam. Starting at narrow end roll up into roll. Sift more icing sugar over outside of roll and place seam side down on towel. Fold towel over top. Store in plastic bag or container. If using other filling, roll up towel with cake and cool. Prepare filling, spread over unrolled cake and roll up again without the towel.

**RASPBERRY SAUCE**

| | | |
|---|---|---|
| Frozen raspberries with juice, thawed and sieved | 15 oz. | 425 g |
| Cornstarch | 1 tbsp. | 15 mL |

*(continued on next page)*

Whisk both ingredients together in saucepan. Place over medium heat. Stir until it boils and thickens. Cool thoroughly. Fill center of plate with sauce. Set slice of jelly roll in center or put large section of roll in center of sauce. Slice and spoon some sauce over each slice.

Pictured on page 71.

# MAPLE NUT CHIFFON

*Very light with a delicious nutty maple flavor. Excellent.*

| | | |
|---|---|---|
| All-purpose flour | 2 cups | 500 mL |
| Brown sugar, packed | 3/4 cup | 175 mL |
| Granulated sugar | 3/4 cup | 175 mL |
| Baking powder | 1 tbsp. | 15 mL |
| Salt | 1 tsp. | 5 mL |
| Cooking oil | 1/2 cup | 125 mL |
| Egg yolks, room temperature | 5 | 5 |
| Water | 3/4 cup | 175 mL |
| Maple flavoring | 2 tsp. | 10 mL |
| Egg whites, room temperature | 1 cup | 250 mL |
| Cream of tartar | 1/2 tsp. | 2 mL |
| Finely chopped walnuts | 1 cup | 250 mL |

Preheat oven to 325°F (160°C). Wash angel food tube pan in hot soapy water to ensure it is totally grease-free. Sift first 5 ingredients into bowl. Make a well in center.

Put next 4 ingredients into well. Set aside. Don't beat yet.

Beat egg whites and cream of tartar until very stiff. Set aside.

Using same beaters, beat egg yolk-flour mixture until smooth. Fold 1/4 at a time gently into egg whites.

Add walnuts. Fold in. Pour into ungreased 10 inch (25 cm) angel food tube pan. Bake in oven for 60 to 70 minutes until an inserted wooden pick comes out clean. Invert pan until cake has cooled.

# ANGEL FOOD

*Light as a feather! Contains no fat.*

| | | |
|---|---|---|
| Sifted cake flour | 1 cup | 225 mL |
| Icing (confectioner's) sugar | ³/₄ cup | 175 mL |
| Egg whites, room temperature at least 2 days old (about 12) | 1¹/₂ cups | 350 mL |
| Salt | ¹/₄ tsp. | 1 mL |
| Cream of tartar | 1¹/₂ tsp. | 7 mL |
| Vanilla | 1 tsp. | 5 mL |
| Almond flavoring | ¹/₄ tsp. | 1 mL |
| Granulated sugar | 1 cup | 225 mL |

Preheat oven to 375°F (190°C). Wash angel food tube pan in hot soapy water to ensure it is totally grease-free. Put flour and icing sugar into sifter. Sift together three times. Use 2 pieces of waxed paper for easy clean up. Set aside.

In mixing bowl beat egg whites and salt on high speed until frothy.

Add cream of tartar, vanilla and almond flavoring. Beat until soft peaks form. Peaks should be soft enough so they bend over slightly at the tips.

Sprinkle 1 tbsp. (15 mL) granulated sugar at a time over egg whites continuing to beat until stiff.

Sift about ¹/₄ flour-sugar mixture over top. Using flat spatula fold into egg whites. Use from 10 to 15 fold-over motions, just enough so dry ingredients are combined. Repeat using ¹/₄ dry mixture each time. Pour into ungreased 10 inch (25 cm) angel food tube pan. Gently cut through batter with knife to remove air pockets. Bake in oven for about 30 to 35 minutes until an inserted wooden pick comes out clean. Invert pan to cool for 1 hour. This cake needs no icing but to fancy it up quickly and without adding sweetness, the frosting that follows is ideal.

## LEMON CHEESE ICING

| | | |
|---|---|---|
| Whipping cream (or 1 envelope topping) | 1 cup | 250 mL |
| Lemon cheese | ¹/₄ cup | 60 mL |

Beat cream until stiff. Add lemon cheese. More or less can be used as your taste dictates. Beat to mix. Spread over top and sides of cake. Chill unless using right away. Makes a fantastic icing.

*(continued on next page)*

**CONFETTI ANGEL FOOD:** Fold 3 tbsp. (50 mL) trim-ettes (hundreds and thousands) into batter before turning into tube pan. These are tiny little colored pellets used for cake decorating. Ice with Pink Butter Icing, page 150.

Pictured on page 17.

# CHOCOLATE CHIFFON CAKE

*This has a very fine texture and a tender crumb. Excellent choice.*

| | | |
|---|---|---|
| Cocoa | 1/2 cup | 125 mL |
| Boiling water | 3/4 cup | 175 mL |
| Sifted cake flour | 1 3/4 cups | 425 mL |
| Granulated sugar | 1 3/4 cups | 425 mL |
| Baking soda | 1 1/2 tsp. | 7 mL |
| Salt | 1 tsp. | 5 mL |
| Cooking oil | 1/2 cup | 125 mL |
| Egg yolks, room temperature | 7 | 7 |
| Vanilla | 2 tsp. | 10 mL |
| Egg whites, room temperature | 7 | 7 |
| Cream of tartar | 1/2 tsp. | 2 mL |

Preheat oven to 325°F (160°C). Wash angel food tube pan in hot soapy water to ensure it is totally grease-free. Stir cocoa and boiling water together in small bowl until smooth. Cool.

Sift flour, sugar, baking soda and salt into mixing bowl. Make a well in center.

Add cooking oil, egg yolks, vanilla and cocoa mixture to well. Set aside. Don't beat yet.

Beat egg whites with cream of tartar in large bowl until very stiff. A path will remain when spatula is drawn through. Set aside.

Using same beaters, beat egg yolk-flour mixture until smooth. Pour about 1/4 at a time over egg whites. Fold in with rubber spatula. Do not stir. Pour into ungreased 10 inch (25 cm) angel food tube pan. Bake in oven for about 55 to 65 minutes until an inserted wooden pick comes out clean. Invert pan until cool.

# MOCHA CHIFFON CAKE

*This yummy cake has specks of chocolate throughout. A light moist cake.*

| | | |
|---|---|---|
| Sifted cake flour | 2¹/₄ cups | 525 mL |
| Granulated sugar | 1¹/₂ cups | 350 mL |
| Baking powder | 1 tbsp. | 15 mL |
| Salt | 1 tsp. | 5 mL |
| Instant coffee granules | 1 tbsp. | 15 mL |
| Hot water | ³/₄ cup | 175 mL |
| Cooking oil | ¹/₂ cup | 125 mL |
| Egg yolks, room temperature | 5 | 5 |
| Vanilla | 1 tsp. | 5 mL |
| Egg whites, room temperature | 1 cup | 225 mL |
| Cream of tartar | ¹/₂ tsp. | 2 mL |
| Semisweet baking chocolate squares, shaved thinly with vegetable peeler | 3 × 1 oz. | 3 × 28 g |

Preheat oven to 325°F (160°C). Wash angel food tube pan in hot soapy water to ensure it is totally grease-free. Sift first 4 ingredients into bowl. Make a well in center.

Dissolve coffee in hot water. Cool.

Put cooking oil, egg yolks, vanilla and cooled coffee into well. Set aside. Don't beat yet.

Beat egg whites and cream of tartar until very stiff. Set aside.

Using same beaters, beat egg yolk-flour mixture until smooth. Fold ¹/₄ at a time gently into egg whites. Add shaved chocolate. Fold in. Pour into ungreased 10 inch (25 cm) angel food tube pan. Bake in oven for 60 to 70 minutes. Invert pan until cake has cooled. Frost if desired with Mocha Fluff, page 147.

Pictured on page 89.

*Ideal for a spring tea. A delicate cake with a delicate pale yellow and white color combination. A touch of yellow food coloring may be added if the yellow is too pale.*

| | | |
|---|---|---|
| **Egg whites, room temperature** | **10** | **10** |
| **Cream of tartar** | **1 tsp.** | **5 mL** |
| **Salt** | **1/2 tsp.** | **2 mL** |
| **Granulated sugar** | **1 1/4 cups** | **300 mL** |
| **Sifted cake flour** | **3/4 cup** | **175 mL** |
| **Egg yolks, beaten** | **6** | **6** |
| **Orange extract** | **1/2 tsp.** | **2 mL** |
| **Sifted cake flour** | **1/2 cup** | **125 mL** |
| **Vanilla** | **1 tsp.** | **5 mL** |

Preheat oven to 350°F (180°C). Wash angel food tube pan in hot soapy water to ensure it is totally grease-free. Beat egg whites until frothy. Add cream of tartar and salt. Beat until stiff.

Fold in sugar. Divide batter in half.

To 1/2 batter fold in first amount of cake flour, egg yolks and orange extract.

To second 1/2 batter fold in remaining flour and vanilla. Place about 1 cup (250 mL) batter at a time, alternating colors, into ungreased 10 inch (25 cm) angel food tube pan. Bake in oven for 30 minutes. Reduce heat to 325°F (160°C) for 20 minutes until an inserted wooden pick comes out clean. Invert pan until cool. Remove and ice with Lemon Cheese Frosting, page 141, making 1/2 recipe.

Pictured on page 89.

*Little Jackie didn't bother to look out for the worms in the apples. He thought he'd let the worms look out for themselves.*

# CHIFFON CAKE

*One of the first cakes of its kind. A favorite of my children for many birthday parties.*

| | | |
|---|---|---|
| Sifted cake flour | 2 cups | 450 mL |
| Granulated sugar | 1¹/₂ cups | 350 mL |
| Baking powder | 1 tbsp. | 15 mL |
| Salt | 1 tsp. | 5 mL |
| Cooking oil | ¹/₂ cup | 125 mL |
| Egg yolks, room temperature | 7 | 7 |
| Cold water | ³/₄ cup | 175 mL |
| Vanilla | 2 tsp. | 10 mL |
| Lemon flavoring | 1 tsp. | 5 mL |
| Egg whites, room temperature | 7 | 7 |
| Cream of tartar | ¹/₂ tsp. | 2 mL |

Preheat oven to 325°F (160°C). Wash angel food tube pan in hot soapy water to ensure it is totally grease-free. Measure flour, sugar, baking powder and salt into sifter. Sift into bowl. Make a well.

Add next 5 ingredients to well in order given. Set aside. Don't beat.

In large mixing bowl beat egg whites and cream of tartar until very stiff. Set aside.

Using same beaters, beat egg yolk-flour mixture until smooth and light. Pour gradually over egg whites, folding in with rubber spatula. Do not stir. Pour into ungreased 10 inch (25 cm) angel food tube pan. Bake in oven for 55 minutes. Increase heat to 350°F (180°C) and bake 10 to 15 minutes more until an inserted wooden pick comes out clean. Invert pan until cool. Frost with Pink Butter Icing, page 150.

# TRUE SPONGE CAKE

*Pale lemon in color this is light and airy. Contains no shortening or leavening agents.*

| | | |
|---|---|---|
| Egg whites, room temperature | 6 | 6 |
| Salt | ¹/₈ tsp. | 0.5 mL |
| Granulated sugar | 1 cup | 250 mL |
| Egg yolks, room temperature | 6 | 6 |
| Lemon juice | 1 tbsp. | 15 mL |
| Grated lemon rind | 1 tsp. | 5 mL |
| Sifted cake flour | 1 cup | 250 mL |

*(continued on next page)*

Preheat oven to 325°F (160°C). Wash angel food tube pan in hot soapy water to ensure it is totally grease-free. Beat egg whites and salt in mixing bowl until soft peaks form.

Sprinkle with about 2 tbsp. (30 mL) sugar at a time beating continually until sugar is dissolved and stiff peaks form. Set aside.

In small mixing bowl beat egg yolks, lemon juice and lemon rind until very thick. A thick ribbon should fall from beaters when raised. Transfer to large mixing bowl. Carefully and gently fold in egg whites.

Sift cake flour 3 more times. Sift ¼ flour at a time over batter. Gently fold in until no trace of white remains. Immediately turn into ungreased 10 inch (25 cm) angel food tube pan. Bake in oven for 55 to 60 minutes until an inserted wooden pick comes out clean. Invert pan to cool for about 1 hour.

## GINGERBREAD

*Quick and easy. Just measure everything into one bowl and beat.*

| | | |
|---|---|---|
| All-purpose flour | 2 cups | 500 mL |
| Granulated sugar | ½ cup | 125 mL |
| Baking powder | 1 tsp. | 5 mL |
| Baking soda | ½ tsp. | 2 mL |
| Salt | 1 tsp. | 5 mL |
| Ginger | 2 tsp. | 10 mL |
| Cinnamon | 1 tsp. | 5 mL |
| Butter or margarine, softened | ½ cup | 125 mL |
| Eggs | 2 | 2 |
| Fancy molasses | ¾ cup | 175 mL |
| Milk | ½ cup | 125 mL |

Preheat oven to 350°F (180°C). Measure all 11 ingredients into mixing bowl. Beat slowly to combine together. Beat at medium high speed for 2 minutes until smooth. Spread into greased 9 × 13 inch (22 × 33 cm) pan. Bake in oven for about 30 minutes until an inserted wooden pick comes out clean. Frost with whipped cream, Snow White Icing, page 148 or Peanut Butter Icing, page 141.

# ORANGE CHIFFON CAKE

*A most popular variation of chiffon cake. Very fine texture. Makes a large cake.*

| | | |
|---|---|---|
| Sifted cake flour | 2¹/₄ cups | 525 mL |
| Granulated sugar | 1¹/₂ cups | 350 mL |
| Baking powder | 1 tbsp. | 15 mL |
| Salt | 1 tsp. | 5 mL |
| Egg yolks, room temperature | 5 | 5 |
| Cooking oil | ¹/₂ cup | 125 mL |
| Prepared orange juice | ³/₄ cup | 175 mL |
| Grated orange rind | 1 tbsp. | 15 mL |
| Vanilla | 1 tsp. | 5 mL |
| Egg whites, room temperature | 1 cup | 225 mL |
| Cream of tartar | ¹/₂ tsp. | 2 mL |

Preheat oven to 325°F (160°C). Wash angel food tube pan in hot soapy water to ensure it is totally grease-free. Sift flour, sugar, baking powder and salt together into bowl. Make a well in center.

Put next 5 ingredients into well. Set aside. Don't beat yet.

Beat egg whites and cream of tartar in mixing bowl until very stiff. Set aside.

Using same beaters, beat egg yolk-flour mixture until smooth. Gently fold ¹/₄ at a time into egg whites. Pour into ungreased 10 inch (25 cm) angel food tube pan. Bake in oven for 60 to 70 minutes until an inserted wooden pick comes out clean. Invert pan until cake has cooled. Remove from pan. Serve plain or frost with Orange Icing, page 150.

*Men who accompany women shopping are better known as wait-watchers.*

# BURNT SUGAR CHIFFON

*Absolutely luscious. Be sure you have burnt sugar syrup on hand.*

| | | |
|---|---|---|
| Sifted cake flour | 2 cups | 450 mL |
| Granulated sugar | 1¹/₂ cups | 350 mL |
| Baking powder | 1 tbsp. | 15 mL |
| Salt | 1 tsp. | 5 mL |
| Cooking oil | ¹/₂ cup | 125 mL |
| Egg yolks, room temperature | 7 | 7 |
| Water | ¹/₄ cup | 50 mL |
| Vanilla | 1 tsp. | 5 mL |
| Burnt Sugar Syrup, page 137 | ¹/₂ cup | 125 mL |
| Egg whites, room temperature | 7 | 7 |
| Cream of tartar | ¹/₂ tsp. | 2 mL |

Preheat oven to 325°F (160°C). Wash angel food tube pan in hot soapy water to ensure it is totally grease-free. Sift flour, sugar, baking powder and salt into medium mixing bowl. Make a well in center.

Add the next 5 ingredients to the well. Set aside. Don't beat yet.

Beat egg whites and cream of tartar in large mixing bowl until very stiff.

Using same beaters, beat egg yolk-flour mixture until smooth and light. Add about ¹/₄ at a time to beaten egg whites folding in with rubber spatula after each addition. Pour into ungreased 10 inch (25 cm) angel food tube pan. Bake in oven for 55 minutes. Increase heat to 350°F (180°C) and bake 10 to 15 minutes more until an inserted wooden pick comes out clean. Invert pan until cool.

*First you doctor a drink and then you nurse it for an hour.*

# PRUNE CAKE

*Moist and spicy. Extra nice with a glaze but also good without.*

| | | |
|---|---|---|
| Eggs | 3 | 3 |
| Granulated sugar | 1¹/₂ cups | 375 mL |
| Cooking oil | 1 cup | 250 mL |
| Chopped cooked prunes (or use baby food) | 1 cup | 250 mL |
| All-purpose flour | 2 cups | 500 mL |
| Baking powder | 1 tsp. | 5 mL |
| Baking soda | 1 tsp. | 5 mL |
| Salt | ¹/₂ tsp. | 2 mL |
| Cinnamon | 1 tsp. | 5 mL |
| Nutmeg | 1 tsp. | 5 mL |
| Cloves | ¹/₄ tsp. | 1 mL |
| Buttermilk | 1 cup | 250 mL |
| Chopped walnuts | 1 cup | 250 mL |

Preheat oven to 350°F (180°C). Beat eggs in mixing bowl. Add remaining ingredients. Mix together. Beat until smooth for about 2 minutes. Pour into greased and floured 12 cup (2.7 L) bundt pan. Bake in oven for about 1 hour until an inserted wooden pick comes out clean. Ice with Brown Sugar Glaze, page 146.

1. Pineapple Upside Down Cake page 91
2. Blueberry Streusel page 50
3. Sour Cream Coffee Cake page 46

# BURNT SUGAR ANGEL FOOD

*A terrific combination. Great flavor and light, light.*

| | | |
|---|---|---|
| Sifted cake flour | 1 cup | 225 mL |
| Icing (confectioner's) sugar | 1/2 cup | 125 mL |
| Egg whites, room temperature (about 12) | 11/2 cups | 350 mL |
| Cream of tartar | 11/2 tsp. | 7 mL |
| Salt | 1/4 tsp. | 1 mL |
| Granulated sugar | 1 cup | 225 mL |
| Burnt Sugar Syrup, see page 137 | 3 tbsp. | 50 mL |
| Vanilla | 1 tsp. | 5 mL |
| Maple flavoring | 1/4 tsp. | 1 mL |

Preheat oven to 375°F (190°C). Wash angel food tube pan in hot soapy water to ensure it is totally grease-free. Sift flour and icing sugar together 3 times. Use waxed paper or plates to sift onto. Set aside.

In mixing bowl beat egg whites, cream of tartar and salt until soft peaks form.

Gradually beat in granulated sugar until stiff.

Add burnt sugar syrup, vanilla and maple flavoring. Beat briefly to mix.

Sift 1/4 flour mixture over at a time. Fold in using rubber spatula. Turn into ungreased 10 inch (25 cm) angel food tube pan. Cut through batter gently with knife to remove any air pockets. Bake in oven for 35 to 40 minutes until an inserted wooden pick comes out clean. Invert to cool for 1 hour. Needs no icing, but if desired ice with Burnt Sugar Icing, page 150 or Caramel Icing, page 138.

*Paré Pointer*

*They tried to get the piano tuner on their baseball team because he had perfect pitch.*

# CHOCOLATE JELLY ROLL

*The eggs are beaten all together in this roll. A snap to make.*

| | | |
|---|---|---|
| Eggs, room temperature | 4 | 4 |
| Granulated sugar | 3/4 cup | 175 mL |
| Vanilla | 1 tsp. | 5 mL |
| All-purpose flour | 3/4 cup | 175 mL |
| Cocoa | 1/4 cup | 60 mL |
| Baking powder | 1 tsp. | 5 mL |
| Salt | 1/4 tsp. | 1 mL |

**Icing (confectioner's) sugar**

Grease 10 × 15 inch (25 × 38 cm) jelly roll pan. Line bottom with waxed paper. Preheat oven to 350°F (180°C).

Beat eggs in small mixing bowl until thick and lemon colored. Add sugar in 3 additions beating well. Mix in vanilla. Transfer to large mixing bowl for better and easier addition of flour.

Sift flour, cocoa, baking powder and salt over batter about 1/3 at a time. Gently fold in. Pour into prepared pan. Bake in oven for about 12 to 15 minutes until an inserted wooden pick comes out clean.

Sift icing sugar or cocoa heavily over tea towel. Invert cake onto towel. Carefully remove waxed paper. Trim crisp edges if any. Roll up from short side along with towel. Cool. Unroll. Spread with filling. Roll without towel. Filling can be slices of ice cream, whipped cream or Mocha Cream Filling, page 149.

*Girls need to keep on their toes to outsmart heels.*

*A moist cake, medium brown in color. It is scrumptious with it's caramel topping.*

| | | |
|---|---|---|
| Boiling water | 1¹/₂ cups | 375 mL |
| Oatmeal | 1 cup | 250 mL |
| Butter or margarine, softened | ¹/₂ cup | 125 mL |
| Brown sugar, packed | 1 cup | 250 mL |
| Granulated sugar | 1 cup | 250 mL |
| Eggs | 2 | 2 |
| Vanilla | 1 tsp. | 5 mL |
| All-purpose flour | 1¹/₂ cups | 375 mL |
| Baking soda | 1 tsp. | 5 mL |
| Cinnamon | 1 tsp. | 5 mL |
| Nutmeg | ¹/₂ tsp. | 2 mL |
| Salt | ¹/₄ tsp. | 1 mL |

**BROILED TOPPING**

| | | |
|---|---|---|
| Butter or margarine | 6 tbsp. | 100 mL |
| Brown sugar, packed | ³/₄ cup | 175 mL |
| Cream | 3 tbsp. | 50 mL |
| Coconut | ³/₄ cup | 175 mL |
| Chopped nuts | ³/₄ cup | 175 mL |
| Vanilla | ¹/₂ tsp. | 2 mL |

Preheat oven to 350°F (180°C). Pour boiling water over oatmeal in bowl. Set aside.

Cream butter and both sugars together well. Beat in eggs 1 at a time. Add vanilla. Stir.

Add flour, baking soda, cinnamon, nutmeg and salt. Mix. Stir in oatmeal mixture. Turn into greased 9 × 13 inch (22 × 33 cm) pan. Bake in oven for 30 to 35 minutes until an inserted wooden pick comes out clean. Put on topping.

**Broiled Topping:** Measure all 6 ingredients into saucepan. Heat and stir to melt butter and dissolve sugar. Spread over warm cake. Broil 6 to 8 inches from heat until browned and bubbly.

Pictured on page 107.

# RAISIN SHEET CAKE

*Cinnamon and raisins plus great icing make this a kid's special. Good for snacks or lunches.*

| | | |
|---|---|---|
| Raisins or currants | 1 cup | 250 mL |
| Instant coffee granules | 1 tsp. | 5 mL |
| Cinnamon | 1 tsp. | 5 mL |
| Boiling water | $3/4$ cup | 175 mL |
| Butter or margarine, softened | $1/2$ cup | 125 mL |
| Granulated sugar | 1 cup | 250 mL |
| Eggs | 2 | 2 |
| Vanilla | 1 tsp. | 5 mL |
| All-purpose flour | $1^1/2$ cups | 375 mL |
| Baking powder | $1/2$ tsp. | 3 mL |
| Baking soda | $1/2$ tsp. | 2 mL |
| Salt | $1/2$ tsp. | 2 mL |

Preheat oven to 350°F (180°C). Combine first 4 ingredients in bowl. Let stand until cooled.

In mixing bowl cream butter and sugar together. Beat in eggs 1 at a time. Mix in vanilla.

Combine flour, baking powder, baking soda and salt in small bowl. Add alternately with raisin mixture. Spread in greased 10 × 15 inch (25 × 38 cm) jelly roll pan. Bake in oven for 20 to 25 minutes until an inserted wooden pick comes out clean. Ice while hot.

**NUTTY ICING**

| | | |
|---|---|---|
| Butter or margarine | $1/2$ cup | 125 mL |
| Milk | $1/4$ cup | 60 mL |
| Instant coffee granules | 1 tsp. | 5 mL |
| Icing (confectioner's) sugar, sifted | 3 cups | 700 mL |
| Vanilla | 1 tsp. | 5 mL |
| Chopped pecans or walnuts (optional) | $1/2$ cup | 125 mL |

Heat butter, milk and coffee granules in medium saucepan. Bring to a boil. Remove from heat.

Add icing sugar, vanilla and nuts. Mix well. Pour over hot cake.

*Just like a fruitcake. Excellent. Makes a large cake but it will disap-pear quickly.*

| | | |
|---|---|---|
| Cooking oil | 1 cup | 225 mL |
| Granulated sugar | 1 cup | 225 mL |
| Brown sugar | 1 cup | 225 mL |
| Eggs | 4 | 4 |
| Finely grated carrot | 3 cups | 675 mL |
| All-purpose flour | 2¹/₂ cups | 575 mL |
| Baking powder | 2 tsp. | 10 mL |
| Baking soda | 1 tsp. | 5 mL |
| Cinnamon | 2 tsp. | 10 mL |
| Salt | 1 tsp. | 5 mL |
| Raisins | 1 cup | 225 mL |
| Candied cherries, halved | 1 cup | 225 mL |
| Candied mixed fruit | 1 cup | 225 mL |
| Chopped dates | 1 cup | 225 mL |
| Coarsely chopped walnuts | 1 cup | 225 mL |
| All-purpose flour | ¹/₂ cup | 125 mL |

Preheat oven to 325°F (160°C). Beat cooking oil with sugars. Beat in eggs 1 at a time. Stir in carrot.

Add next 5 ingredients. Stir to moisten.

Add raisins, cherries, mixed fruit, dates and walnuts to second amount of flour. Stir to coat. Add to batter. Stir. Turn into greased and floured 10 inch (25 cm) angel food tube pan or 12 cup (2.7 L) bundt pan. Bake in oven until an inserted wooden pick comes out clean, about 1¹/₂ hours.

*Sometimes the more things one has done to be ashamed of, the more respectable one is.*

# TOMATO SOUP CAKE

*An old family favorite without nuts and raisins. Cake is fairly thin which means some icing with each bite. Moist.*

| | | |
|---|---|---|
| Butter or margarine | 1/2 cup | 125 mL |
| Granulated sugar | 1 cup | 250 mL |
| Egg | 1 | 1 |
| All-purpose flour | 1 1/2 cups | 375 mL |
| Cinnamon | 1/2 tsp. | 2 mL |
| Nutmeg | 1/2 tsp. | 2 mL |
| Cloves | 1/2 tsp. | 2 mL |
| Salt | 1/2 tsp. | 2 mL |
| Raisins (optional) | 1 cup | 250 mL |
| Chopped walnuts (optional) | 3/4 cup | 175 mL |
| Baking soda | 1 tsp. | 5 mL |
| Hot water | 2 tsp. | 10 mL |
| Tomato soup | 10 oz. | 284 mL |

Preheat oven to 325°F (160°C). Cream butter and sugar together in mixing bowl. Add egg and beat well.

Measure flour, cinnamon, nutmeg, cloves, salt, raisins and walnuts into separate bowl. Mix thoroughly.

Mix baking soda with hot water. Stir into tomato soup. Add to butter mixture in 2 parts alternately with flour mixture in 3 parts, beginning and ending with flour. Scrape into greased 9 × 13 inch (22 × 33 cm) pan. Bake in oven for 35 to 45 minutes until an inserted wooden pick comes out clean. Cool. Frost with Simple Chocolate Icing, page 148 or Cream Cheese Icing, page 145.

Pictured on page 125.

# PINEAPPLE CARROT CAKE

*You will find this lighter than most carrot cakes. Very tasty.*

| | | |
|---|---|---|
| Granulated sugar | 1 cup | 250 mL |
| All-purpose flour | 1 1/2 cups | 325 mL |
| Baking powder | 1 tsp. | 5 mL |
| Baking soda | 1 tsp. | 5 mL |
| Cinnamon | 1 tsp. | 5 mL |
| Salt | 1/2 tsp. | 2 mL |

*(continued on next page)*

| | | |
|---|---|---|
| Cooking oil | 2/3 cup | 150 mL |
| Eggs | 2 | 2 |
| Finely grated carrot | 1 cup | 250 mL |
| Crushed pineapple with juice | 1/2 cup | 125 mL |
| Vanilla | 1 tsp. | 5 mL |

Preheat oven to 350°F (180°C). Measure first six ingredients into mixing bowl. Mix.

Add rest of ingredients in order given. Mix slowly to moisten. Beat for 2 minutes at medium speed. Spread in greased 9 × 9 inch (22 × 22 cm) pan. Bake in oven for 35 minutes until an inserted wooden pick comes out clean. Cool and frost with Cream Cheese Icing, page 145.

# ZUCCHINI CAKE

*Moist with a mild spice flavor.*

| | | |
|---|---|---|
| All-purpose flour | 2 1/2 cups | 625 mL |
| Baking powder | 2 tsp. | 10 mL |
| Baking soda | 1 tsp. | 5 mL |
| Salt | 1 tsp. | 5 mL |
| Cinnamon | 2 tsp. | 10 mL |
| Cloves | 1/2 tsp. | 2 mL |
| Eggs | 3 | 3 |
| Cooking oil | 1/2 cup | 125 mL |
| Granulated sugar | 1 1/3 cups | 325 mL |
| Prepared orange juice | 1/2 cup | 125 mL |
| Almond flavoring | 1 tsp. | 5 mL |
| Grated zucchini, with peel, squeezed to drain | 1 1/2 cups | 375 mL |

Preheat oven to 350°F (180°C). Measure first 6 ingredients into mixing bowl.

In another bowl beat eggs until frothy. Add cooking oil and sugar. Mix well. Add orange juice, almond flavoring and zucchini. Stir. Add this mixture to dry ingredients. Stir just until moistened. Pour into greased 9 × 13 inch (22 × 33 cm) pan. Bake in oven for 35 to 40 minutes until an inserted wooden pick comes out clean. Cool. Frost with Orange Icing, page 150 or Cream Cheese Icing, page 145.

Pictured with Cream Cheese Icing on page 107.

# CHOCOLATE BEET CAKE

*A dark dark cake, finely textured and chocolaty.*

| | | |
|---|---|---|
| Eggs | 3 | 3 |
| Granulated sugar | 1½ cups | 350 mL |
| Cooking oil | 1 cup | 225 mL |
| Cooked mashed beets | 1½ cups | 350 mL |
| Vanilla | 1 tsp. | 5 mL |
| All-purpose flour | 1¾ cups | 400 mL |
| Cocoa | ½ cup | 125 mL |
| Baking soda | 1½ tsp. | 7 mL |
| Salt | ½ tsp. | 2 mL |

Preheat oven to 350°F (180°C). Beat eggs and sugar together in mixing bowl. Add cooking oil, beets and vanilla. Mix.

Stir in flour, cocoa, baking soda and salt. Stir to moisten. Spread in 2 greased round 8 inch (20 cm) layer pans. Bake in oven for 30 to 35 minutes or until an inserted wooden pick comes out clean. Cool. Ice with Simple Chocolate Icing, page 148 or Chocolate Mint Icing, page 148.

**CHOCO MINT BEET CAKE:** Add ¾ tsp. (4 mL) peppermint flavoring to wet ingredients.

# CARROT CAKE

*Make this your regular carrot cake recipe. Rich color. Rich looking.*

| | | |
|---|---|---|
| Cooking oil | 1 cup | 225 mL |
| Granulated sugar | 1½ cups | 350 mL |
| Eggs | 4 | 4 |
| Grated carrot | 3 cups | 700 mL |
| All-purpose flour | 2 cups | 450 mL |
| Baking soda | 2 tsp. | 10 mL |
| Salt | ½ tsp. | 2 mL |
| Cinnamon | 2 tsp. | 10 mL |
| Chopped walnuts (optional) | ¾ cup | 175 mL |

Preheat oven to 350°F (180°C). Beat cooking oil and sugar together in mixing bowl. Beat in eggs 1 at a time. Stir in carrot.

*(continued on next page)*

Add remaining ingredients. Fold in to moisten. Spread in greased 9 × 13 inch (22 × 33 cm) pan. Bake in oven until an inserted wooden pick comes out clean, about 45 minutes. Spread with Cream Cheese Icing, page 145, when cool.

Pictured on page 125.

# CRUMB CAKE

*This spice cake has a topping baked with the cake. Very good.*

| | | |
|---|---|---|
| **All-purpose flour** | **2 cups** | **500 mL** |
| **Butter or margarine** | **³/₄ cup** | **175 mL** |
| **Granulated sugar** | **1 cup** | **250 mL** |
| **Sour milk, see Note** | **1 cup** | **250 mL** |
| **Baking soda** | **1 tsp.** | **5 mL** |
| **Egg, beaten** | **1** | **1** |
| **Cinnamon** | **1 tsp.** | **5 mL** |
| **Nutmeg** | **1 tsp.** | **5 mL** |
| **Cloves** | **1 tsp.** | **5 mL** |
| **Salt** | **¹/₂ tsp.** | **2 mL** |
| **Raisins or currants** | **1 cup** | **250 mL** |
| **Reserved crumbs** | **1 cup** | **250 mL** |

Preheat oven to 350°F (180°C). Measure first 3 ingredients into mixing bowl. Crumble together until mealy. Reserve 1 cup (250 mL) for topping.

Stir sour milk and baking soda together and add to the mixture in mixing bowl.

Add egg, cinnamon, nutmeg, cloves, salt and raisins. Mix together. Spread in greased 9 × 9 inch (22 × 22 cm) pan.

Sprinkle with reserved crumbs. Bake in oven for 35 to 40 minutes until an inserted wooden pick comes out clean.

**Note:** To make sour milk, add milk to 1 tbsp. (15 mL) vinegar in measuring cup. Stir.

# SOUR CREAM COFFEE CAKE

*Everyone likes this with cinnamon and nuts topping it off.*

| | | |
|---|---|---|
| Butter or margarine, softened | 1 cup | 250 mL |
| Granulated sugar | 1¼ cups | 300 mL |
| Eggs | 2 | 2 |
| Sour cream | 1 cup | 250 mL |
| Vanilla | 1 tsp. | 5 mL |
| All-purpose flour | 2 cups | 500 mL |
| Baking powder | 1 tsp. | 5 mL |
| Baking soda | ½ tsp. | 2 mL |
| Salt | ¼ tsp. | 1 mL |
| **TOPPING** | | |
| Brown sugar, packed | ⅔ cup | 150 mL |
| Cinnamon | 1½ tsp. | 7 mL |
| Chopped walnuts | ¾ cup | 175 mL |

Preheat oven to 350°F (180°C). Cream butter and sugar together well. Beat in eggs 1 at a time. Stir in sour cream and vanilla.

Add flour, baking powder, baking soda and salt. Stir to moisten. Put ½ batter into greased 10 inch (25 cm) angel food tube pan.

**Topping:** Mix sugar, cinnamon and walnuts together. Sprinkle ½ over batter in pan. Cover with second ½ batter. Sprinkle with second ½ nut mixture. Bake in oven for about 45 minutes until an inserted wooden pick comes out clean. Let stand for 20 minutes. Turn out of pan turning right side up.

Pictured on page 35.

# BEETNIK

*This cake changes color in the oven. It goes in quite pink and comes out a nice rich beige color. A large cake.*

| | | |
|---|---|---|
| Cooking oil | 1 cup | 225 mL |
| Granulated sugar | 2 cups | 450 mL |
| Eggs | 4 | 4 |
| Vanilla | 1 tsp. | 5 mL |
| Grated raw beets | 2 cups | 450 mL |
| Crushed pineapple with juice | 1 cup | 225 mL |

*(continued on next page)*

| | | |
|---|---|---|
| All-purpose flour | 3 cups | 675 mL |
| Baking powder | 2 tsp. | 10 mL |
| Baking soda | 1 tsp. | 5 mL |
| Cinnamon | 1¹/₂ tsp. | 7 mL |
| Allspice | ¹/₂ tsp. | 2 mL |
| Salt | 1 tsp. | 5 mL |

Preheat oven to 350°F (180°C). Beat cooking oil, sugar and 1 egg together. Beat in rest of eggs 1 at a time. Add vanilla.

Mix in beets and pineapple with juice.

Add remaining ingredients. Stir to moisten. Turn into greased 9 × 13 inch (22 × 33 cm) pan. Bake in oven for about 45 minutes until an inserted wooden pick comes out clean.

## SPICE CAKE

*Just the right spicy taste.*

| | | |
|---|---|---|
| Butter or margarine, softened | ¹/₂ cup | 125 mL |
| Granulated sugar | ³/₄ cup | 175 mL |
| Eggs | 2 | 2 |
| Vanilla | 1 tsp. | 5 mL |
| All-purpose flour | 2 cups | 450 mL |
| Baking powder | 2 tsp. | 10 mL |
| Salt | ¹/₄ tsp. | 1 mL |
| Cinnamon | 2 tsp. | 10 mL |
| Nutmeg | 1 tsp. | 5 mL |
| Allspice | ¹/₂ tsp. | 2 mL |
| Cloves | ¹/₄ tsp. | 1 mL |
| Milk | ³/₄ cup | 175 mL |

Preheat oven to 350°F (180°C). Cream butter with sugar in mixing bowl. Beat in eggs. Add vanilla. Mix.

Mix next 7 ingredients together in small bowl.

Add milk to butter mixture in 2 parts alternately with flour mixture in 3 parts, beginning and ending with flour. Turn into greased 8 × 8 inch (20 × 20 cm) pan. Bake in oven for about 35 to 40 minutes until an inserted wooden pick comes out clean. Ice with Butter Icing, page 150, Simple Chocolate Icing, page 148 or Caramel Icing, page 138.

# BEET AND CARROT CAKE

*Raw vegetables add colorful flecks to this cake.*

| | | |
|---|---|---|
| Cooking oil | 1 cup | 250 mL |
| Granulated sugar | 1¹/₂ cups | 375 mL |
| Eggs | 3 | 3 |
| Vanilla | 1 tsp. | 5 mL |
| Finely grated raw beets | 1 cup | 250 mL |
| Finely grated carrots | 1 cup | 250 mL |
| All-purpose flour | 2 cups | 500 mL |
| Baking powder | 2¹/₂ tsp. | 12 mL |
| Cinnamon | 1 tsp. | 5 mL |
| Salt | ¹/₂ tsp. | 2 mL |
| Chopped walnuts (optional) | ¹/₂ cup | 125 mL |

Preheat oven to 350°F (180°C). Beat cooking oil with sugar in mixing bowl. Beat in eggs 1 at a time. Add vanilla. Stir.

Add beet and carrot. Stir.

Stir in flour, baking powder, cinnamon, salt and walnuts. Spread in greased 9 × 13 inch (22 × 33 cm) pan. Bake in oven for about 45 to 50 minutes until an inserted wooden pick comes out clean.

# RHUBARB COFFEE CAKE

*What spring treat could be better? It is worth inviting company for this alone.*

| | | |
|---|---|---|
| Butter or margarine | ¹/₂ cup | 125 mL |
| Granulated sugar | 1¹/₂ cups | 375 mL |
| Eggs | 2 | 2 |
| Sour cream | 1 cup | 250 mL |
| Vanilla | 1 tsp. | 5 mL |
| All-purpose flour | 2 cups | 500 mL |
| Baking soda | 1 tsp. | 5 mL |
| Finely cut rhubarb | 2 cups | 500 mL |
| **TOPPING** | | |
| Brown sugar, packed | ¹/₂ cup | 125 mL |
| All-purpose flour | 1 tbsp. | 15 mL |
| Cinnamon | 1 tsp. | 5 mL |
| Butter or margarine, softened | 1 tbsp. | 15 mL |

*(continued on next page)*

Preheat oven to 350°F (180°C). Cream butter and sugar together in mixing bowl. Beat in eggs 1 at a time. Stir in sour cream and vanilla.

Mix flour and baking soda together in small bowl. Fold into batter.

Stir in rhubarb. Turn into greased 9 × 13 inch (22 × 33 cm) pan.

**Topping:** Mix all 4 ingredients together until crumbly. Sprinkle over top. Bake in oven for 30 to 40 minutes until an inserted wooden pick comes out clean.

## PUMPKIN CAKE

*Rather a solid pound-type cake, this cuts into many slices.*

| | | |
|---|---|---|
| **Eggs, room temperature** | 4 | 4 |
| **Granulated sugar** | 2 cups | 450 mL |
| **Cooking oil** | 1 cup | 225 mL |
| **Canned pumpkin (without spices)** | 14 oz. | 398 mL |
| **All-purpose flour** | 2 cups | 450 mL |
| **Baking soda** | 2 tsp. | 10 mL |
| **Salt** | 1/2 tsp. | 2 mL |
| **Cinnamon** | 2 tsp. | 10 mL |
| **Cloves** | 1/2 tsp. | 2 mL |
| **Ginger** | 1/2 tsp. | 2 mL |
| **Nutmeg** | 1/2 tsp. | 2 mL |

Preheat oven to 350°F (180°C). Beat eggs in mixing bowl until frothy. Add sugar. Beat until lemony in color and fluffy.

Mix in oil and pumpkin slowly. Beat well.

Add remaining ingredients. Stir until moistened. Turn into greased and floured 10 inch (25 cm) angel food tube pan. Bake in oven for about 1 hour or until an inserted wooden pick comes out clean. Let stand 20 minutes. Remove from pan to rack to cool. Ice with Cream Cheese Icing, page 145.

Paré Pointer

*The blotter industry is a very absorbing industry.*

# BLUEBERRY STREUSEL

*This large cake will feed a coffee crowd. Fresh blueberries are layered under the topping.*

| | | |
|---|---|---|
| All-purpose flour | 3 cups | 700 mL |
| Granulated sugar | 3/4 cup | 175 mL |
| Baking powder | 1 tbsp. | 15 mL |
| Salt | 1 tsp. | 5 mL |
| Cinnamon | 1 1/2 tsp. | 7 mL |
| Nutmeg | 1 tsp. | 5 mL |
| Butter or margarine, softened | 1/2 cup | 125 mL |
| Eggs | 3 | 3 |
| Milk | 1 cup | 225 mL |
| Vanilla | 1 tsp. | 5 mL |
| Blueberries, fresh or frozen | 3 cups | 700 mL |

**TOPPING**

| | | |
|---|---|---|
| All-purpose flour | 2/3 cup | 150 mL |
| Rolled oats | 2/3 cup | 150 mL |
| Brown sugar, packed | 3/4 cup | 175 mL |
| Butter or margarine, softened | 1/2 cup | 125 mL |
| Cinnamon | 1 tsp. | 5 mL |

Preheat oven to 350°F (180°C). Measure first 7 ingredients into mixing bowl. Cut in butter until crumbly.

Add eggs, milk and vanilla. Beat until smooth and thick. Spread into greased 9 × 13 inch (22 × 33 cm) pan.

Sprinkle blueberries over top.

**Topping:** Mix all 5 ingredients together until crumbly. Sprinkle over blueberries. Pat gently with your hand. Bake in oven for 50 to 60 minutes until an inserted wooden pick comes out clean.

Pictured on page 35.

*What a braggart! Every time he opens his mouth he puts in his feats.*

# CHERRY CREAM COFFEE CAKE

*A moist white cake with a pretty red layer beneath a not too sweet topping. In fact you may even want to add more brown sugar when you make it for the second time.*

| | | |
|---|---|---|
| Butter or margarine, softened | 1/2 cup | 125 mL |
| Granulated sugar | 1 cup | 250 mL |
| Eggs | 2 | 2 |
| Sour cream | 1 cup | 250 mL |
| Vanilla | 1 tsp. | 5 mL |
| All-purpose flour | 2 cups | 500 mL |
| Baking powder | 1 1/2 tsp. | 7 mL |
| Baking soda | 1 tsp. | 5 mL |
| Salt | 1/4 tsp. | 1 mL |
| Cherry pie filling | 19 oz. | 540 mL |
| **TOPPING** | | |
| Brown sugar, packed | 1/2 cup | 125 mL |
| All-purpose flour | 3/4 cup | 175 mL |
| Cinnamon | 1 tsp. | 5 mL |
| Butter or margarine, softened | 1/3 cup | 75 mL |
| Salt | 1/4 tsp. | 1 mL |

Preheat oven to 350°F (180°C). Cream butter and sugar together. Beat in eggs 1 at a time. Mix in sour cream and vanilla.

Sift in flour, baking powder, baking soda and salt. Mix to moisten. Scrape into greased 9 × 13 inch (22 × 33 cm) pan. Use wet hand to pat smooth.

Spread pie filling over top.

**Topping:** Mix all 5 ingredients together until crumbly. Sprinkle over pie filling. Bake in oven for 40 to 45 minutes until an inserted wooden pick comes out clean. Best served hot.

*How can you get a parking ticket in a large city when you can't find a place to park?*

# GENOESE SPONGE

*This cake has a fairly firm texture. A nice buttery color.*

| | | |
|---|---|---|
| Egg whites, room temperature | 6 | 6 |
| Cream of tartar | 1/2 tsp. | 2 mL |
| Granulated sugar | 3/4 cup | 175 mL |
| Butter or margarine, softened (butter is best) | 1 cup | 250 mL |
| Granulated sugar | 1 cup | 250 mL |
| Egg yolks, room temperature | 6 | 6 |
| Sifted cake flour | 2 cups | 500 mL |
| Baking powder | 1/2 tsp. | 2 mL |
| Salt | 1/2 tsp. | 2 mL |

Preheat oven to 350°F (180°C). Beat egg whites and cream of tartar in mixing bowl until soft peaks form.

Add sugar gradually, beating until very stiff.

In medium mixing bowl, using same beaters, cream butter and sugar well. Add egg yolks. Beat until thick and fluffy.

Sift flour, baking powder and salt over batter. Fold in. Gently fold in egg whites. Pour into greased 10 inch (25 cm) angel food tube pan. Bake in oven for 50 to 60 minutes until an inserted wooden pick comes out clean. Cool. Ice with Snow White Icing, page 148, Simple Chocolate Icing, page 148 or Coffee Icing, page 150.

# DUTCH APPLE CAKE

*Apple slices are layered over top of the batter and covered with a crumb mixture. Serve with whipped cream for a sure hit.*

| | | |
|---|---|---|
| Butter or margarine, softened | ½ cup | 125 mL |
| Granulated sugar | ¼ cup | 60 mL |
| Egg | 1 | 1 |
| Brandy flavoring | 1½ tsp. | 7 mL |
| All-purpose flour | 1¼ cups | 300 mL |
| Baking powder | 1½ tsp. | 7 mL |
| Salt | ½ tsp. | 2 mL |
| Milk | ⅔ cup | 150 mL |
| Cooking apples, peeled, cut in eighths | 3-4 | 3-4 |
| **TOPPING** | | |
| Butter or margarine, melted | 3 tbsp. | 50 mL |
| Brown sugar, or granulated sugar | ½ cup | 125 mL |
| All-purpose flour | ¼ cup | 60 mL |
| Cinnamon | 1 tsp. | 5 mL |

Preheat oven to 375°F (190°C). Cream butter with sugar and egg until smooth. Add flavoring.

Mix flour, baking powder and salt in small bowl.

Add flour mixture to margarine mixture in 3 parts alternately with milk in 2 parts, beginning and ending with flour mixture. Spread in greased 8 x 8 inch (20 x 20 cm) pan.

Arrange apple slices in rows over top to cover.

**Topping:** Mix all ingredients together. Sprinkle over apples. Bake in oven for about 30 minutes or until apples are tender. Serve warm or cold.

*Paré Pointer*

*When an anxious mother asked how many children get homesick, the camp director said only the ones who have dogs or cats.*

# PRALINE CHEESECAKE

*A creamy rich, nutty, butterscotch flavor. Complete with a flavored sour cream topping.*

## CRUST

| | | |
|---|---|---|
| Butter or margarine | 1/4 cup | 60 mL |
| Graham cracker crumbs | 1 cup | 250 mL |
| Brown sugar, packed | 3 tbsp. | 50 mL |
| Chopped pecans or walnuts | 1/3 cup | 75 mL |

## FILLING

| | | |
|---|---|---|
| Cream cheese, softened | 2 × 8 oz. | 2 × 250 g |
| Dark brown sugar, packed | 1 1/4 cups | 300 mL |
| Eggs | 3 | 3 |
| Rum flavoring | 1 tsp. | 5 mL |
| Vanilla | 1 tsp. | 5 mL |
| Sour cream | 1/4 cup | 60 mL |
| Chopped pecans or walnuts | 1/3 cup | 75 mL |

## TOPPING

| | | |
|---|---|---|
| Sour cream | 1 1/2 cups | 350 mL |
| Brown sugar, packed | 1/4 cup | 60 mL |
| Maple flavoring | 3/4 tsp. | 4 mL |
| Rum flavoring | 1/2 tsp. | 2 mL |

Whipped cream, for garnish
Pecan halves, for garnish

Preheat oven to 350°F (180°C).

**Crust:** Melt butter in small saucepan. Stir in graham crumbs, brown sugar and pecans. Pack into ungreased 9 to 9 1/2 inch (22 to 24 cm) springform pan. Set aside.

**Filling:** Beat cream cheese and brown sugar together well until smooth and fluffy. Slowly beat in eggs 1 at a time just until blended. Add rum flavoring, vanilla, sour cream and pecans. Stir. Pour into prepared pan. Bake in oven for about 55 to 60 minutes until set. Remove to cake rack while you prepare topping.

**Topping:** Stir together sour cream, brown sugar and both flavorings. Spread over cheesecake. Return to 350°F (180°C) oven. Bake for 10 minutes. Loosen sides of cake. Cool until almost room temperature then chill for a few hours or overnight before serving.

To serve, put a dollop of sweetened whipped cream on each slice. Add at least 1 pecan or better yet add a few.

# CHOCOLATE CHEESECAKE

*Your very wish come true. Yogurt never tasted so good.*

| | | |
|---|---|---|
| Butter or margarine | 1/4 cup | 50 mL |
| Graham cracker crumbs | 1 cup | 250 mL |
| Cocoa | 2 tbsp. | 30 mL |
| Granulated sugar | 2 tbsp. | 30 mL |
| Semisweet baking chocolate squares, cut up | 6 × 1 oz. | 6 × 28 g |
| Cream cheese, softened | 2 × 8 oz. | 2 × 250 g |
| Granulated sugar | 1 cup | 250 mL |
| Eggs | 3 | 3 |
| Vanilla | 1 1/2 tsp. | 7 mL |
| Yogurt | 1 cup | 250 mL |
| **TOPPING** | | |
| Semisweet chocolate baking squares, cut up | 3 × 1 oz. | 3 × 28 g |
| Heavy cream or evaporated milk | 2 tbsp. | 30 mL |

Preheat oven to 325°F (160°C). Melt butter in small saucepan over medium heat. Stir in crumbs, cocoa and first amount of sugar. Pack into bottom of 8 inch (20 cm) springform pan. Set aside.

Melt chocolate in heavy pan over low heat. Stir often.

Beat cream cheese and second amount of sugar together in medium bowl until light and fluffy. Beat in eggs 1 at a time at low speed just to blend. Mix in vanilla.

Add melted chocolate and yogurt. Mix until no streaks remain. Pour into prepared pan. Bake in oven for about 1 hour and 10 minutes until set. Loosen edges and cool.

**Topping:** Combine chocolate and cream in small saucepan over low heat. Stir often until melted. Cool slightly. Smooth over cheesecake. Chill several hours or overnight before serving.

# BLITZ TORTE

*A good white cake with a meringue topping sandwiched with a cream filling.*

| | | |
|---|---|---|
| Butter or margarine, softened | 1/2 cup | 125 mL |
| Granulated sugar | 2/3 cup | 150 mL |
| Egg yolks | 4 | 4 |
| Vanilla | 1 tsp. | 5 mL |
| All-purpose flour | 1 1/4 cups | 275 mL |
| Baking powder | 1 tsp. | 5 mL |
| Salt | 1/4 tsp. | 1 mL |
| Milk | 1/3 cup | 75 mL |

**MERINGUE TOPPING**

| | | |
|---|---|---|
| Egg whites, room temperature | 4 | 4 |
| Vinegar | 1 tbsp. | 15 mL |
| Granulated sugar | 3/4 cup | 175 mL |
| Finely chopped walnuts | 1/2 cup | 125 mL |

Preheat oven to 325°F (160°C). Cream butter and sugar together in mixing bowl. Beat in egg yolks until fluffy. Mix in vanilla.

Stir flour, baking powder and salt together in small bowl.

Add flour mixture to butter mixture in 3 parts alternately with milk in 2 parts, beginning and ending with flour. Spread in 2 greased round 8 inch (20 cm) layer pans. Set aside.

**Meringue Topping:** Beat egg whites until soft peaks form. Add vinegar. Beat in sugar gradually. Beat until stiff. Spread over batter in pans.

Sprinkle with walnuts. Bake in oven for about 40 minutes until an inserted wooden pick comes out clean. Cool. Fill with Cream Filling.

**CREAM FILLING**

| | | |
|---|---|---|
| Milk | 1 cup | 250 mL |
| Granulated sugar | 1/4 cup | 60 mL |
| All-purpose flour | 3 tbsp. | 50 mL |
| Salt | 1/4 tsp. | 1 mL |
| Egg | 1 | 1 |
| Vanilla | 1/2 tsp. | 2 mL |

*(continued on next page)*

Heat milk in saucepan over medium heat.

Stir sugar, flour and salt together in small bowl. Add egg and vanilla. Mix well. When milk begins to boil, add egg mixture while stirring continually. Stir until it returns to a boil and is thickened. Remove from heat. Cool. Spread over layer, meringue side down. Put second layer, meringue side up over filling. Refrigerate before serving.

# CHOCOLATE MOCHA CAKE

*A one bowl cake that makes a good layer cake. Ice with Coffee Icing for color contrast.*

| | | |
|---|---|---|
| All-purpose flour | 2 cups | 500 mL |
| Granulated sugar | 2 cups | 500 mL |
| Cocoa | $\frac{2}{3}$ cup | 150 mL |
| Cooking oil | $\frac{1}{2}$ cup | 125 mL |
| Eggs | 2 | 2 |
| Sour milk or buttermilk, see Note | 1 cup | 250 mL |
| Baking soda | 1 tsp. | 5 mL |
| Baking powder | 1 tsp. | 5 mL |
| Salt | $\frac{1}{2}$ tsp. | 2 mL |
| Instant coffee granules | 1 tbsp. | 15 mL |
| Hot water | $\frac{3}{4}$ cup | 175 mL |

Preheat oven to 350°F (180°C). Measure first 9 ingredients into mixing bowl.

Dissolve instant coffee in hot water. Add to mixing bowl. Beat at medium speed for 2 minutes until smooth. Batter will be thin. Pour into 2 greased 8 inch (20 cm) layer pans. Bake in oven for 45 minutes until an inserted wooden pick comes out clean. Let stand 10 minutes. Turn out onto racks to cool. Ice with Coffee Icing, page 150.

**Note:** To make sour milk, add milk to 1 tbsp. (15 mL) vinegar in measuring cup. Stir.

Pictured on cover.

# SACHER TORTE

*A dense chocolate cake. If you can't get to Vienna, enjoy this famous SAH-ker Torte here.*

| | | |
|---|---|---|
| Butter or margarine, softened | 1/2 cup | 125 mL |
| Granulated sugar | 1/2 cup | 125 mL |
| Egg yolks, room temperature | 6 | 6 |
| Vanilla | 1 tsp. | 5 mL |
| Semisweet baking chocolate squares, melted | 6 × 1 oz. | 6 × 28 g |
| All-purpose flour | 3/4 cup | 175 mL |
| Salt | 1/4 tsp. | 1 mL |
| Egg whites, room temperature | 6 | 6 |
| **TOPPING** | | |
| Apricot jam, sieved | 1/4 cup | 50 mL |
| Semisweet baking chocolate squares, cut up | 3 × 1 oz. | 3 × 28 g |
| Butter or margarine | 2 tbsp. | 30 mL |

Preheat oven to 350°F (180°C). Cream butter in mixing bowl until fluffy. Beat in sugar gradually. Beat in egg yolks, beating until light colored. Add vanilla. Mix.

Mix in melted chocolate. Add flour and salt. Slowly mix in.

Beat egg whites until stiff. Fold into batter. Turn into greased 9 inch (22 cm) springform pan. Bake in oven for 35 to 40 minutes until an inserted wooden pick comes out clean. Cool.

**Topping:** Heat apricot jam and press through sieve. Spread over top of cake. If you would rather, slice cake to make 2 layers putting jam between layers as well. You will need more jam.

Melt chocolate and butter in pan over hot water. Have water hot but don't allow it to boil. Cool to lukewarm so it isn't too runny. Pour over cake and spread over sides.

*A delight to see as well as to eat. If pecans aren't available walnuts or hazelnuts may be used.*

| | | |
|---|---|---|
| **Egg whites, room temperature** | 6 | 6 |
| **Egg yolks** | 6 | 6 |
| **Granulated sugar** | $^2/_3$ **cup** | 150 mL |
| **Vanilla** | $^1/_2$ **tsp.** | 2 mL |
| **Instant coffee granules, crushed** | $^1/_2$ **tsp.** | 2 mL |
| **All-purpose flour** | $^1/_2$ **cup** | 125 mL |
| **Cocoa** | 1 tsp. | 5 mL |
| **Ground pecans** | 1$^1/_2$ **cups** | 350 mL |

Preheat oven to 350°F (180°C). Beat egg whites in mixing bowl until stiff. Set aside.

In smaller bowl beat egg yolks well. Add sugar, vanilla and coffee. Beat well. Fold into egg whites.

Gently fold in flour and cocoa. Add pecans and fold in. Spread in 2 greased round 8 inch (20 cm) layer pans. Bake in oven for about 25 minutes until an inserted wooden pick comes out clean. Cool. Remove from pan. Turn right side up. Fill and frost.

## MOCHA CREAM FILLING AND FROSTING

| | | |
|---|---|---|
| **Whipping cream (or 2 envelopes topping)** | 2 cups | 500 mL |
| **Granulated sugar** | 2 tbsp. | 30 mL |
| **Instant coffee granules** | 1 tbsp. | 15 mL |
| **Boiling water** | 1 tbsp. | 15 mL |
| **Pecan halves for garnish** | | |

Beat cream and sugar together in mixing bowl until stiff.

Dissolve coffee granules in boiling water. Cool. Add to cream. Beat in. Spread between layers and on top and sides. Edges of tops may be trimmed to flatten before frosting if needed as they tend to be higher around the outside.

Garnish with pecan halves. Keep chilled until ready to serve.

Pictured on page 107.

# DEVIL'S FOOD

*A finely textured chocolate cake. Good with a date filling. A jam filling is good too.*

| | | |
|---|---|---|
| Sifted cake flour | 2 cups | 500 mL |
| Baking soda | 1 tsp. | 5 mL |
| Salt | 1/4 tsp. | 1 mL |
| Butter or margarine, softened | 1/2 cup | 125 mL |
| Brown sugar, packed | 1 1/4 cups | 300 mL |
| Eggs | 2 | 2 |
| Unsweetened baking chocolate squares, melted | 3 × 1 oz. | 3 × 28 g |
| Vanilla | 1 tsp. | 5 mL |
| Milk | 1 cup | 250 mL |

Preheat oven to 350°F (180°C). Sift measured flour, baking soda and salt together 3 times. Set aside.

Cream butter until fluffy in mixing bowl. Add sugar. Beat well. Beat in eggs 1 at a time. Add melted chocolate and vanilla. Beat well.

Add milk to butter mixture in 2 parts alternately with flour mixture in 3 parts, beginning and ending with flour. Divide batter between 2 greased round 8 inch (20 cm) layer pans. Bake in oven for about 25 to 30 minutes until an inserted wooden pick comes out clean. Cool. Fill with Date Filling, page 138. Ice with Simple Chocolate Icing, page 148.

# NO EGG CHOCOLATE CAKE

*Sometimes known as Wacky or Crazy Cake, this is a one bowl cake. Beat everything together and bake. Moist with a fine texture.*

| | | |
|---|---|---|
| All-purpose flour | 3 cups | 750 mL |
| Granulated sugar | 2 cups | 500 mL |
| Cocoa | 1/2 cup | 125 mL |
| Baking soda | 2 tsp. | 10 mL |
| Salt | 1 tsp. | 5 mL |
| Cooking oil | 3/4 cup | 175 mL |
| Vinegar | 2 tsp. | 10 mL |
| Vanilla | 2 tsp. | 10 mL |
| Water | 2 cups | 500 mL |

*(continued on next page)*

Preheat oven to 350°F (180°C). Measure first 5 ingredients into mixing bowl. Stir. Make a well in the center.

Add remaining ingredients to well. Mix until smooth. Pour into greased 9 × 13 inch (22 × 33 cm) pan. Bake in oven for 35 to 40 minutes until an inserted wooden pick comes out clean. Cool.

## ORANGE CHOCOLATE CAKE

*This light colored chocolate cake is rich with orange flavor. An excellent cake.*

| | | |
|---|---|---|
| Prepared orange juice | 1/2 cup | 125 mL |
| Semisweet chocolate chips | 1 cup | 250 mL |
| Butter or margarine, softened | 1 cup | 250 mL |
| Granulated sugar | 2 cups | 500 mL |
| Eggs | 4 | 4 |
| Vanilla | 1 tsp. | 5 mL |
| Baking soda | 1 tsp. | 5 mL |
| Prepared orange juice | 1 cup | 250 mL |
| All-purpose flour | 2 1/2 cups | 625 mL |
| Salt | 1/2 tsp. | 2 mL |
| Grated orange rind | 2 tbsp. | 30 mL |

Preheat oven to 350°F (180°C). Put first amount of orange juice and chocolate chips into small saucepan over medium heat. Stir often to hasten melting.

In mixing bowl cream butter and sugar. Beat in eggs 1 at a time. Add vanilla. Beat until fluffy. Add chocolate mixture.

Stir baking soda into second amount of orange juice.

Combine flour, salt and orange rind. Add to butter mixture in 3 parts alternately with baking soda-juice mixture in 2 parts, beginning and ending with dry ingredients. Spread in 3 greased 9 inch (22 cm) layer pans. Bake in oven for 25 to 30 minutes until an inserted wooden pick comes out clean.

# CHOCOLATE ZUCCHINI CAKE

*A moist cake and a good keeper. This one is self-iced but if you prefer an icing simply omit the chocolate chips.*

| | | |
|---|---|---|
| Butter or margarine, softened | 1/2 cup | 125 mL |
| Granulated sugar | 1 3/4 cups | 425 mL |
| Eggs | 2 | 2 |
| Cooking oil | 1/2 cup | 125 mL |
| Sour milk (or 1 tbsp., 15 mL vinegar, plus milk) | 1/2 cup | 125 mL |
| Vanilla | 1 tsp. | 5 mL |
| Grated zucchini with peel | 2 cups | 500 mL |
| All-purpose flour | 2 1/2 cups | 625 mL |
| Cocoa | 1/3 cup | 75 mL |
| Baking soda | 1 tsp. | 5 mL |
| Baking powder | 1/2 tsp. | 2 mL |
| Cinnamon | 1/2 tsp. | 2 mL |
| Salt | 1/2 tsp. | 2 mL |
| Semisweet chocolate chips | 3/4 cup | 150 mL |

Preheat oven to 350°F (180°C). In large mixing bowl cream butter and sugar together well. Beat in eggs 1 at a time. Mix in cooking oil, sour milk, vanilla and zucchini.

Mix next 6 ingredients together in small bowl. Add to batter. Stir to moisten. Spread in greased 9 × 13 inch (22 × 33 cm) pan.

Sprinkle with chocolate chips. Bake in oven for about 35 minutes until an inserted wooden pick comes out clean.

# CHOCO MAYO CAKE

*In this chocolate cake, mayonnaise is substituted for the butter. Good.*

| | | |
|---|---|---|
| All-purpose flour | 2 cups | 500 mL |
| Granulated sugar | 1 cup | 250 mL |
| Cocoa | 1/4 cup | 60 mL |
| Baking soda | 2 tsp. | 10 mL |
| Salt | 1/4 tsp. | 1 mL |
| Mayonnaise | 1 cup | 250 mL |
| Water | 1 cup | 250 mL |
| Vanilla | 1 tsp. | 5 mL |

*(continued on next page)*

Preheat oven to 350°F (180°C). Measure ingredients into mixing bowl in order given. Mix together well. Spread in greased 9 × 13 inch (22 × 33 cm) pan. Bake in oven for about 30 to 35 minutes until an inserted wooden pick comes out clean.

## DARK CHOCOLATE CAKE

*This has a nice fine crumb. Made in three layers, it lends itself to be considered an elegant cake.*

| | | |
|---|---|---|
| Boiling water | 2 cups | 500 mL |
| Cocoa | 1 cup | 250 mL |
| All-purpose flour | 2³/₄ cups | 675 mL |
| Baking soda | 2 tsp. | 10 mL |
| Baking powder | ¹/₂ tsp. | 2 mL |
| Salt | ¹/₂ tsp. | 2 mL |
| Butter or margarine, softened | 1 cup | 250 mL |
| Granulated sugar | 2¹/₄ cups | 500 mL |
| Eggs | 4 | 4 |
| Vanilla | 1¹/₂ tsp. | 7 mL |

Preheat oven to 350°F (180°C). Pour boiling water over cocoa in medium bowl. Whisk until smooth. Cool.

Sift flour, baking soda, baking powder and salt onto plate.

In mixing bowl cream butter and sugar together well. Beat in eggs 1 at a time beating until light colored. Add vanilla.

Add flour mixture to butter mixture in 3 parts alternately with cocoa mixture in 2 parts, beginning and ending with flour. Spread into 3 greased 9 inch (22 cm) round pans. Bake in oven for 25 to 30 minutes until an inserted wooden pick comes out clean. Cool. Ice with Chocolate Cheese Icing, page 145. More melted chocolate chips or cocoa may be added to make a darker icing.

Pictured on page 143.

# CRATER CAKE

*This Cola Cake contains tiny marshmallows that rise to the top and melt while cake bakes leaving crusty little craters. May be iced if desired or eaten as is.*

| | | |
|---|---|---|
| All-purpose flour | 2 cups | 500 mL |
| Granulated sugar | 2 cups | 500 mL |
| Butter or margarine | 1 cup | 250 mL |
| Cocoa | 3 tbsp. | 50 mL |
| Cola carbonated beverage | 1 cup | 250 mL |
| Buttermilk | 1/2 cup | 125 mL |
| Eggs, beaten | 2 | 2 |
| Baking soda | 1 tsp. | 5 mL |
| Vanilla | 1 tsp. | 5 mL |
| Salt | 1/2 tsp. | 2 mL |
| Miniature marshmallows | 2 cups | 500 mL |

Preheat oven to 350°F (180°C). Measure flour and sugar into mixing bowl. Stir.

Put butter, cocoa and cola into saucepan over medium heat. Stir and bring to a boil. Pour over flour-sugar mixture. Mix well.

Add buttermilk, beaten eggs, baking soda, vanilla and salt. Stir to combine.

Mix in marshmallows. Spread in greased 9 × 13 inch (22 × 33 cm) pan. Bake in oven for about 35 to 40 minutes until an inserted wooden pick comes out clean. Cool and ice with Cola Frosting.

## COLA FROSTING

| | | |
|---|---|---|
| Butter or margarine | 1/4 cup | 60 mL |
| Cocoa | 3 tbsp. | 50 mL |
| Cola carbonated beverage | 1/3 cup | 75 mL |
| Icing (confectioner's) sugar | 2 cups | 450 mL |
| Chopped pecans or walnuts | 1/2 cup | 125 mL |
| Vanilla | 1 tsp. | 5 mL |

Combine butter, cocoa and cola in medium saucepan. Heat over medium heat to the boiling point. Remove from heat.

Stir in icing sugar, pecans and vanilla. Add more cola or icing sugar as needed to make a not too thick icing. Pour over warm cake. Makes about 1 1/2 cups (350 mL).

# CHIP AND DATE CAKE

*Covered with chocolate chips and nuts, this is a feast for the eyes.*
*Just meant for lunch boxes. Baked and iced in one step.*

| | | |
|---|---|---|
| Chopped dates | 1 cup | 250 mL |
| Boiling water | 1 cup | 250 mL |
| Baking soda | 1 tsp. | 5 mL |
| Butter or margarine, softened | 1 cup | 250 mL |
| Granulated sugar | 1 cup | 250 mL |
| Eggs | 2 | 2 |
| Vanilla | 1 tsp. | 5 mL |
| All-purpose flour | 1³/₄ cups | 425 mL |
| Cocoa | 3 tbsp. | 50 mL |
| Salt | ¹/₂ tsp. | 2 mL |
| Semisweet chocolate chips | 1 cup | 250 mL |
| Chopped walnuts | ¹/₂ cup | 125 mL |

Preheat oven to 350°F (180°C). Put dates, water and baking soda into medium bowl. Cool.

Cream butter and sugar together in mixing bowl. Beat in eggs 1 at a time. Stir in vanilla.

Add flour, cocoa and salt alternately with date mixture. Spread in greased 9 × 13 inch (22 × 33 cm) pan.

Sprinkle with chocolate chips and walnuts. Bake in oven for about 35 to 45 minutes until an inserted wooden pick comes out clean.

Pictured on page 125.

*One gossip to another: "I have to tell you this right now before I find out it isn't true."*

# CHOCOLATE CREAM CHEESE CAKE

*Fabulous flavor.*

**FILLING**

| | | |
|---|---|---|
| Cream cheese, softened | 8 oz. | 250 g |
| Eggs | 2 | 2 |
| Granulated sugar | 1/2 cup | 125 mL |
| Cornstarch | 1 tbsp. | 15 mL |
| Vanilla | 1/2 tsp. | 2 mL |

**CAKE**

| | | |
|---|---|---|
| Butter or margarine, softened | 1/2 cup | 125 mL |
| Granulated sugar | 2 cups | 500 mL |
| Eggs | 2 | 2 |
| Vanilla | 1 tsp. | 5 mL |
| All-purpose flour | 2 cups | 500 mL |
| Baking powder | 1 tsp. | 5 mL |
| Baking soda | 1/2 tsp. | 2 mL |
| Salt | 1 tsp. | 5 mL |
| Milk | 1 1/3 cups | 325 mL |
| Unsweetened baking chocolate squares, melted | 4 × 1 oz. | 4 × 28 g |

Preheat oven to 350°F (180°C).

**Filling:** Beat cheese and 1 egg well. Beat in second egg. Add sugar, cornstarch and vanilla. Beat. Set aside.

**Cake:** Cream butter and sugar together well. Beat in eggs 1 at a time. Add vanilla.

Stir flour, baking powder, baking soda and salt together in bowl.

Add flour mixture in 3 parts alternately with milk in 2 parts, beginning and ending with flour.

Stir in melted chocolate. Pour 1/2 batter into greased 9 × 13 inch (22 × 33 cm) pan. Put dabs of cream cheese mixture over top. Smooth. Put dabs of remaining cake batter here and there over cheese mixture. Smooth as best you can. Bake in oven 50 to 60 minutes until an inserted wooden pick comes out clean. Cool. Frost with Chocolate Cheese Icing, page 145.

**Variation:** Add about 1/2 cup (125 mL) chopped maraschino cherries that have been very well drained to filling.

Pictured on page 107.

*Rich in both color and flavor. Chocolate can't be detected. Dusting with powdered sugar would be enough to serve or if you'd like an icing, a brown sugar or a butter icing would be good.*

| | | |
|---|---|---|
| Butter or margarine, softened | 1/2 cup | 125 mL |
| Granulated sugar | 1 cup | 250 mL |
| Eggs | 2 | 2 |
| Vanilla | 1 tsp. | 5 mL |
| All-purpose flour | 2 cups | 500 mL |
| Cocoa | 2 tbsp. | 30 mL |
| Cinnamon | 2 tsp. | 10 mL |
| Baking soda | 1 tsp. | 5 mL |
| Salt | 1/2 tsp. | 2 mL |
| Cooked, chopped prunes (or use baby food) | 1 cup | 250 mL |
| Buttermilk | 1/2 cup | 125 mL |

Preheat oven to 350°F (180°C). Beat butter in mixing bowl until fluffy. Beat in sugar. Add eggs 1 at a time beating well after each addition. Mix in vanilla.

Mix next 5 dry ingredients together in small bowl.

Combine prunes and buttermilk. Add flour mixture to butter mixture in 3 parts alternately with prunes and buttermilk in 2 parts, beginning and ending with flour. Pour into greased 9 × 9 inch (22 × 22 cm) pan. Bake in oven for about 35 to 45 minutes until an inserted wooden pick comes out clean.

Paré Pointer

*If you see a rabbit chasing a grasshopper, what you are fully seeing is Hopalong Grassidy.*

# CHOCOLATE OATMEAL CAKE

*Would you serve this for breakfast? Good.*

| | | |
|---|---|---|
| Boiling water | 1 cup | 250 mL |
| Oatmeal | 1 cup | 250 mL |
| Butter or margarine, cut up | 1/2 cup | 125 mL |
| Eggs, beaten | 2 | 2 |
| Brown sugar, packed | 1 1/4 cups | 300 mL |
| Vanilla | 1 tsp. | 5 mL |
| All-purpose flour | 1 cup | 250 mL |
| Cocoa | 1/4 cup | 60 mL |
| Baking powder | 1 tsp. | 5 mL |
| Baking soda | 1 tsp. | 5 mL |
| Salt | 1/2 tsp. | 2 mL |

Preheat oven to 350°F (180°C). Pour boiling water over oatmeal and butter in mixing bowl. Let stand 10 minutes. Stir occasionally.

Stir in eggs, sugar and vanilla.

Stir remaining ingredients together in small bowl and add. Mix well. Pour into greased 8 × 8 inch (20 × 20 cm) pan. Bake in oven for 30 to 40 minutes until an inserted wooden pick comes out clean.

1. Jelly Roll with Raspberry Sauce
   page 24
2. Fruit Flan page 104

# CHOCOLATE POTATO CAKE

*An easy use for leftover mashed potato.*

| | | |
|---|---|---|
| Butter or margarine, softened | 1 cup | 225 mL |
| Granulated sugar | 2 cups | 450 mL |
| Eggs | 4 | 4 |
| Mashed potato | 1 cup | 225 mL |
| Unsweetened baking chocolate squares, melted | 3 × 1 oz. | 3 × 28 g |
| All-purpose flour | 2 cups | 450 mL |
| Baking powder | 1 tsp. | 5 mL |
| Baking soda | 1/2 tsp. | 2 mL |
| Cinnamon | 1 tsp. | 5 mL |
| Nutmeg | 1/2 tsp. | 2 mL |
| Allspice | 1/2 tsp. | 2 mL |
| Salt | 1/4 tsp. | 1 mL |
| Sour cream | 1 cup | 225 mL |
| Chopped walnuts (optional) | 1 cup | 225 mL |
| Chopped dates (optional) | 1 cup | 225 mL |

Preheat oven to 350°F (180°C). Cream butter and sugar until fluffy in mixing bowl. Beat in eggs 1 at a time. Add potato. Mix in. Add chocolate. Beat until smooth.

Measure next 7 ingredients into small bowl. Stir.

Add flour mixture to butter mixture in 3 parts alternately with sour cream in 2 parts, beginning and ending with flour.

Stir in walnuts and dates. Spread in greased 9 × 13 inch (22 × 33 cm) pan. Bake in oven for about 40 to 45 minutes until an inserted wooden pick comes out clean.

*There is still one bargain left nowadays. Gossip is dirt cheap.*

# BLACK FOREST CAKE

*A showpiece. Chocolate layers, chocolate cream and cherries make a dessert almost too stunning to cut into.*

| | | |
|---|---|---|
| Eggs, room temperature | 6 | 6 |
| Granulated sugar | 1 cup | 225 mL |
| All-purpose flour | 3/4 cup | 175 mL |
| Cocoa | 1/2 cup | 125 mL |
| Butter or margarine, melted and cooled | 1/2 cup | 125 mL |
| Vanilla | 1 tsp. | 5 mL |

Preheat oven to 350°F (180°C). Beat eggs in mixing bowl until frothy. Gradually add sugar beating until light colored and thick.

Sift flour and cocoa over batter 1/2 at a time. Gently fold in after each addition.

Fold butter and vanilla in gradually. Divide batter among 3 greased round 8 inch (20 cm) pans. Bake in oven for about 15 to 20 minutes until an inserted wooden pick comes out clean. Let stand for 5 to 10 minutes. Turn out onto racks to cool.

## FILLING

| | | |
|---|---|---|
| Canned cherries, drained, reserve juice and a few whole cherries for top garnish | 2 × 14 oz. | 2 × 398 mL |
| Kirsch liqueur or sherry (or alcohol-free sherry) | 1/4 cup | 50 mL |
| Reserved cherry juice | | |
| Cornstarch | 2 tbsp. | 30 mL |
| Granulated sugar | 2 tbsp. | 30 mL |
| Lemon juice | 1 tsp. | 5 mL |

## WHIPPED CREAM

| | | |
|---|---|---|
| Whipping cream (or 2 envelopes topping) | 2 cups | 500 mL |
| Cocoa | 1/4 cup | 60 mL |
| Granulated sugar | 2 tbsp. | 30 mL |
| Vanilla | 1 tsp. | 5 mL |

*(continued on next page)*

## ICING

| | | |
|---|---|---|
| Butter or margarine, softened | 1/4 cup | 60 mL |
| Icing (confectioner's) sugar | 2 cups | 450 mL |
| Cocoa | 1/2 cup | 125 mL |
| Prepared coffee or water | 1/4 cup | 60 mL |

## CHOCOLATE CURLS

| | | |
|---|---|---|
| Semisweet baking chocolate square | 1 | 1 |

**Filling:** After draining cherries remove the whole cherries for garnish and cut the rest in half, removing stones. Reserve 15 to 20 halves to press into icing rims.

Sprinkle kirsch over cake layers. Use more if you like.

Put cherry juice, cornstarch, sugar and lemon juice into small saucepan. Whisk together over medium heat until it boils and thickens. Cool. Stir in cherry halves.

**Whipped Cream:** Beat cream in mixing bowl until fairly thick. Add cocoa, sugar and vanilla. Beat until stiff.

**Icing:** Mix all ingredients together well adding small amounts of icing sugar or coffee as needed to make proper consistency for piping. Now pipe a rim of icing around outside edge of 1 cake layer on serving plate. Spoon 1/2 thickened cherries in center. Press a few cherry halves down slightly in icing rim. Spoon about 1/3 whipped cream over top. Repeat with second layer. Spread remaining icing on third layer and place on top. Cover with remaining 1/3 whipped cream. Garnish with whole cherries arranged in a circle.

**Chocolate Curls:** Warm chocolate square slightly. Using vegetable peeler, peel chocolate forming curls. Put these in center of cherries.

Pictured on page 143.

*Relationships come and go but chocolate is forever.*

# JIFFY CHOCOLATE CAKE

*For a quick treat warm or cold this is an old favorite. Just put everything into one bowl to beat. A cinch. Has a tender clingy crumb.*

| | | |
|---|---|---|
| All-purpose flour | 1¼ cups | 300 mL |
| Granulated sugar | 1 cup | 250 mL |
| Cocoa | ¼ cup | 60 mL |
| Butter or margarine, softened | ¼ cup | 60 mL |
| Baking powder | 1 tsp. | 5 mL |
| Baking soda | 1 tsp. | 5 mL |
| Salt | ½ tsp. | 2 mL |
| Egg | 1 | 1 |
| Vanilla | 1 tsp. | 5 mL |
| Hot water | 1 cup | 250 mL |

Preheat oven to 350°F (180°C). In mixing bowl measure all ingredients in order given. Beat until smooth. Pour into greased 8 or 9 inch (20 or 22 cm) square pan. Double recipe to fill 9 × 13 inch (22 × 33 cm) pan. Bake in oven for 30 to 40 minutes until an inserted wooden pick comes out clean.

# MISSISSIPPI MUD CAKE

*Looks muddy - the kind you can eat. Similar to a cakey brownie with gooey marshmallow under a chocolate icing. Great!*

**CAKE**

| | | |
|---|---|---|
| Butter or margarine | 1 cup | 250 mL |
| Cocoa | ½ cup | 125 mL |
| Granulated sugar | 2 cups | 500 mL |
| Eggs | 4 | 4 |
| All-purpose flour | 1½ cups | 375 mL |
| Baking powder | 1 tsp. | 5 mL |
| Salt | ½ tsp. | 2 mL |
| Chopped pecans or walnuts | 1½ cups | 375 mL |
| Vanilla | 1 tsp. | 5 mL |

**TOPPING**

| | | |
|---|---|---|
| Jar of marshmallow cream (or use large marshmallows, cut in half), to cover | 7 oz. | 200 g |

*(continued on next page)*

## ICING

| | | |
|---|---|---|
| Butter or margarine, softened | 1/4 cup | 60 mL |
| Cocoa | 1/3 cup | 75 mL |
| Milk | 1/2 cup | 125 mL |
| Icing (confectioner's) sugar | 3 cups | 750 mL |
| Vanilla | 1 tsp. | 5 mL |

Preheat oven to 350°F (180°C).

**Cake:** Heat butter and cocoa in large saucepan over low heat. Stir often. Remove from heat.

Add sugar. Beat well. Beat in eggs 1 at a time.

Stir in flour, baking powder and salt.

Add pecans and vanilla to batter. Stir. Pour into greased 9 × 13 inch (22 × 33 cm) pan. Bake in oven for about 35 to 45 minutes until an inserted wooden pick comes out clean.

**Topping:** Spread marshmallow cream over hot cake. If you are using marshmallows, cut large ones in half. Place cut side down and close together. To hasten melting place in oven for a half a minute or so. Watch carefully.

**Icing:** Beat all ingredients together in bowl. Spoon over marshmallow topping while still hot. Spread. Cake will get muddied by the spreading action.

Pictured on page 107.

*Everyone is aware of the three secrets of public speaking. Be sincere, be brief, be seated.*

# CHOCOLATE SHEET CAKE

*Especially good for kids. Cake is thin so you get some icing with every bite. A lunch box special.*

| | | |
|---|---|---|
| All-purpose flour | 2 cups | 500 mL |
| Granulated sugar | 2 cups | 500 mL |
| Butter or margarine | 1/2 cup | 125 mL |
| Water | 1 cup | 250 mL |
| Cocoa | 1/2 cup | 125 mL |
| Buttermilk or sour cream | 1/2 cup | 125 mL |
| Eggs | 2 | 2 |
| Vanilla | 1 tsp. | 5 mL |
| Baking soda | 1 tsp. | 5 mL |
| Salt | 1/4 tsp. | 1 mL |

Preheat oven to 350°F (180°C). Measure flour and sugar into mixing bowl.

In saucepan heat butter, water and cocoa to boiling point. Pour over flour-sugar mixture. Beat to mix.

Beat in remaining ingredients. Pour into greased 11 × 17 inch (28 × 43 cm) cookie sheet with sides. Bake in oven until an inserted wooden pick comes out clean, about 20 to 25 minutes. Ice with Chocolate Nut Icing while hot.

## CHOCOLATE NUT ICING

| | | |
|---|---|---|
| Butter or margarine | 1/2 cup | 125 mL |
| Cocoa | 1/4 cup | 60 mL |
| Milk | 1/3 cup | 75 mL |
| Icing (confectioner's) sugar, sifted | 3 cups | 700 mL |
| Vanilla | 1 tsp. | 5 mL |
| Chopped walnuts (optional) | 1/2 cup | 125 mL |

Heat butter, cocoa and milk in medium saucepan to the boiling point.

Stir in icing sugar, vanilla and walnuts. Pour immediately over hot cake. It will be runny but will firm up as it cools. Spread slowly from center to outer edges.

**Note:** A 10 × 15 inch (25 × 38 cm) jelly roll pan can be used but it is a bit small. Icing is more apt to run off sides.

# CHERRY CHIP CAKE

*Cherries and chocolate chips look good and taste good together. A fairly solid cake.*

| | | |
|---|---|---|
| Butter or margarine, softened | 1/2 cup | 125 mL |
| Granulated sugar | 2/3 cup | 150 mL |
| Eggs | 2 | 2 |
| Vanilla | 1/2 tsp. | 2 mL |
| Almond flavoring | 1/4 tsp. | 1 mL |
| Chopped candied cherries | 1/3 cup | 75 mL |
| All-purpose flour | 2 cups | 450 mL |
| Baking powder | 1 1/2 tsp. | 7 mL |
| Salt | 1/4 tsp. | 1 mL |
| Milk | 1/4 cup | 60 mL |
| Semisweet chocolate chips | 1/2 cup | 125 mL |

Preheat oven to 350°F (180°C). Cream butter and sugar until fluffy. Beat in eggs 1 at a time until light. Mix in vanilla, almond flavoring and cherries.

Mix flour, baking powder and salt together in small bowl.

Add flour mixture to butter mixture in 2 parts alternately with milk in 1 part, beginning and ending with flour.

Fold in chocolate chips. Spread in greased 8 × 8 inch (20 × 20 cm) cake pan. Bake in oven for about 40 minutes until an inserted wooden pick comes out clean.

# WEDDING CAKE

*If you plan to use a fruitcake as a wedding cake, the following guidelines will be helpful.*

A cake consisting of 3 tiers will require 15 pounds (6.8 kg) of fruitcake batter. Use 3 different sizes of round pans — 6 × 3 inch deep (15 × 7.5 cm), 8 × 3 inch deep (20 × 7.5 cm) and 10 × 3 inch deep (25 × 7.5 cm). Fill each pan 3/4 full. Allow more time for baking according to the size. Recommended fruitcakes are, Easy Light Fruitcake, page 81, Favorite Fruitcake, page 84 and Festive Fruitcake, page 92.

# SOUTHERN PECAN CAKE

*Thoroughly delectable!*

| | | |
|---|---|---|
| **Eggs** | 2 | 2 |
| **Buttermilk** | 1/2 cup | 125 mL |
| **Vanilla** | 1 tsp. | 5 mL |
| **Baking soda** | 1 tsp. | 5 mL |
| **All-purpose flour** | 2 cups | 500 mL |
| **Granulated sugar** | 2 cups | 500 mL |
| **Salt** | 1/2 tsp. | 2 mL |
| **Water** | 1 cup | 250 mL |
| **Butter or margarine** | 1/2 cup | 125 mL |
| **Cooking oil** | 1/2 cup | 125 mL |
| **Cocoa** | 1/4 cup | 60 mL |

Preheat oven to 350°F (180°C). In small bowl beat eggs well. Add buttermilk, vanilla and baking soda. Mix. Set aside.

Measure and stir flour, sugar and salt into mixing bowl. Set aside.

Put remaining 4 ingredients into medium saucepan over medium heat. Bring to a boil. Pour over flour mixture in mixing bowl. Beat until smooth.

Add egg mixture to mixing bowl. Beat well. Pour into greased 9 × 13 inch (22 × 33 cm) pan. Bake in oven for about 30 to 35 minutes until an inserted wooden pick comes out clean. Cool and frost with Pecan Frosting.

**PECAN FROSTING**

| | | |
|---|---|---|
| **Unsweetened baking chocolate squares** | 1 1/2 × 1 oz. | 1 1/2 × 28 g |
| **Butter or margarine** | 1/2 cup | 125 mL |
| **Milk** | 1/4 cup | 60 mL |
| **Vanilla** | 1 tsp. | 5 mL |
| **Icing (confectioner's) sugar** | 3 cups | 750 mL |
| **Chopped pecans** | 1 cup | 250 mL |

Put chocolate, butter, milk and vanilla into large saucepan over medium heat. Bring to a boil stirring often. Remove from heat.

Add icing sugar. Beat well. If preferred, transfer to mixing bowl to beat. Add a bit more milk or icing sugar as needed for proper spreading consistency. Stir in pecans. Spread over cake.

# EASY LIGHT FRUITCAKE

*This will be a must for every time you want a light fruitcake. Excellent. Fruit is very showy. Make a few weeks ahead.*

| | | |
|---|---|---|
| Candied cherries, halved | 1 lb. | 454 g |
| Candied pineapple rings, cut up | 5 | 5 |
| Golden raisins | 2 lbs. | 900 g |
| Cut mixed peel | 1/2 lb. | 225 g |
| Pecans or almonds | 1 cup | 225 mL |
| All-purpose flour | 1 cup | 225 mL |
| Butter or margarine, softened | 1 lb. | 454 g |
| Granulated sugar | 2 cups | 450 mL |
| Eggs | 6 | 6 |
| Prepared orange juice | 1/4 cup | 60 mL |
| Vanilla | 1 tsp. | 5 mL |
| All-purpose flour | 5 cups | 1.12 L |
| Baking powder | 2 tsp. | 10 mL |
| Salt | 1/2 tsp. | 2 mL |
| Almonds, split | 6 | 6 |

Preheat oven to 275°F (140°C). Line bottom and sides of 2 greased 9 × 5 × 3 inch (22 × 12 × 7 cm) loaf pans and 1 round 4¹/₂ inch (11 cm) × 3 inch (7.5 cm) deep pan with brown paper. Grease paper. Set aside. Other size pans may be used. Fill 3/4 full.

Mix first 6 ingredients together well in bowl. Set aside.

Cream butter and sugar together. Beat in eggs 1 at a time. Mix in orange juice and vanilla.

Combine second amount of flour, baking powder and salt. Add and stir. Add floured fruit and mix. Spoon into prepared pans.

Arrange split almonds over top. Bake in oven for about 3 hours until an inserted wooden pick comes out clean. Cover with foil if top gets too dark while baking. Weighs 9 pounds (4 kg).

Pictured on page 53.

# EASY FRUITCAKE

*It is hard to know which is best about this cake, the ease to make it, the economy of it or the goodness of it.*

| | | |
|---|---|---|
| Light raisins | 3/4 cup | 175 mL |
| Dark raisins | 3/4 cup | 175 mL |
| Currants | 1 1/2 cups | 375 mL |
| Butter or margarine | 1/2 cup | 125 mL |
| Granulated sugar | 1 cup | 250 mL |
| Baking soda | 1 tsp. | 5 mL |
| Water | 1 cup | 250 mL |
| Eggs | 2 | 2 |
| All-purpose flour | 2 cups | 500 mL |
| Baking powder | 1 tsp. | 5 mL |
| Salt | 1/4 tsp. | 1 mL |
| Vanilla or almond flavoring | 1 tsp. | 5 mL |

Preheat oven to 325°F (160°C). Measure first seven ingredients into large heavy saucepan. Bring to boil, stirring frequently, over medium heat. Simmer for 15 minutes. Cool.

Add remaining ingredients to cooled mixture. Mix well. Turn into greased 9 × 5 × 3 inch (23 × 12 × 7 cm) loaf pan or 2 pound (1 kg) tin. Bake in oven for about 1 1/2 to 2 hours until an inserted wooden pick comes out clean. Weighs about 2 1/4 pounds (1 kg).

Pictured on page 53.

# CHOCOLATE FUDGE CAKE

*Fairly dark and a very fine smooth texture.*

| | | |
|---|---|---|
| Sifted cake flour | 2 1/4 cups | 550 mL |
| Baking soda | 2 tsp. | 10 mL |
| Salt | 1/2 tsp. | 2 mL |
| Butter or margarine, softened | 1/2 cup | 125 mL |
| Brown sugar, packed | 2 1/2 cups | 625 mL |
| Eggs | 3 | 3 |
| Vanilla | 1 1/2 tsp. | 7 mL |
| Unsweetened baking chocolate squares, melted | 3 × 1 oz. | 3 × 28 g |
| Sour cream | 1 cup | 250 mL |
| Boiling water | 1 cup | 250 mL |

*(continued on next page)*

Preheat oven to 350°F (180°C). Measure flour, baking soda and salt into bowl. Stir. Set aside.

In mixing bowl cream butter and sugar until fluffy. Beat in eggs 1 at a time. Mix in vanilla and melted chocolate.

Add sour cream to butter mixture in 2 parts and flour mixture in 3 parts, beginning and ending with flour.

Stir in boiling water. Turn into 3 greased 8 or 9 inch (20 or 22 cm) round layer pans or 9 × 13 inch (22 × 33 cm) pan. Bake in oven for about 35 minutes until an inserted wooden pick comes out clean. Let stand for 10 minutes. Turn out onto racks to cool.

# SULTANA CAKE

*A slice of this and a cup of tea. Ecstasy!*

| | | |
|---|---|---|
| **Raisins (sultanas)** | 2$^{1}/_{4}$ cups | 500 mL |
| **Water to cover** | | |
| **Butter or margarine, cut up** | 1 cup | 250 mL |
| **Granulated sugar** | 1$^{1}/_{2}$ cups | 350 mL |
| **Eggs** | 3 | 3 |
| **Lemon flavoring** | $^{1}/_{2}$ tsp. | 2 mL |
| **All-purpose flour** | 2$^{3}/_{4}$ cups | 625 mL |
| **Baking powder** | 1 tsp. | 5 mL |
| **Salt** | $^{1}/_{4}$ tsp. | 1 mL |

Preheat oven to 350°F (180°C). Cover raisins with water in medium saucepan. Bring to a boil over medium heat. Boil for 5 minutes. Drain.

Add butter and sugar to raisins. Beat thoroughly with spoon.

Add eggs 1 at a time. Spoon-beat after each addition. Add lemon flavoring.

Combine flour, baking powder and salt. Add and mix well with other ingredients. Line 9 inch (22 cm) round × 3 inch (7.5 cm) deep cake pan with greased paper. Scrape batter into prepared pan. Bake in oven for about 1 hour until an inserted wooden pick comes out clean. An 8 × 8 inch (20 × 20 cm) pan will take about 65 to 70 minutes. Start testing for doneness sooner if using tube pan as it will cook faster. Needs no icing.

Pictured on page 53.

# FAVORITE FRUITCAKE

*A medium color cake. Not dark. Not light. Fruity and good. Make a few weeks ahead.*

| | | |
|---|---|---|
| Golden raisins | 1 lb. | 454 g |
| Whole candied cherries | 3/4 lb. | 350 g |
| Candied pineapple, cut up | 3/4 lb. | 350 g |
| Cut candied orange peel | 1/4 lb. | 125 g |
| Cut candied lemon peel | 1/4 lb. | 125 g |
| Blanched almonds, halved | 1/4 lb. | 125 g |
| Pecan halves or walnuts | 1/4 lb. | 125 g |
| All-purpose flour | 1/2 cup | 125 mL |
| Butter or margarine, softened | 1 cup | 225 mL |
| Brown sugar, packed | 2 cups | 450 mL |
| Eggs | 4 | 4 |
| All-purpose flour | 2 1/2 cups | 600 mL |
| Baking powder | 1 tsp. | 5 mL |
| Salt | 1 tsp. | 5 mL |
| Cinnamon | 1 tsp. | 5 mL |
| Apple jelly or raspberry | 1/2 cup | 125 mL |
| Milk | 1/2 cup | 125 mL |
| Vanilla | 1 tsp. | 5 mL |
| Instant coffee granules dissolved in equal amount of hot water (optional) | 1 tbsp. | 15 mL |

Preheat oven to 300°F (150°C). Line bottom and sides of 2 loaf pans, 9 × 5 × 3 inch (22 × 12 × 7 cm), with foil. Grease foil well. Strips of greased brown paper may also be used.

Measure first eight ingredients into bowl. Stir well to coat with flour. Set aside.

Beat butter and sugar together in large mixing bowl. Beat in eggs 1 at a time.

Put second amount of flour, baking powder, salt and cinnamon into another bowl. Stir.

Combine last four ingredients in bowl. Stir.

Add flour mixture in 3 parts alternately with jelly, milk, vanilla and coffee mixture in 2 parts. Mix well. Add fruit mixture. Stir together.

*(continued on next page)*

Spoon into prepared pans. Bake in oven for 2¹/₂ to 3 hours. Cake may be covered with brown paper during last hour of baking to prevent tops from browning too much. An inserted wooden pick should come out clean. Cool cake in pans, then wrap in foil or plastic. Freezes well. Weighs about 6¹/₂ pounds (3 kg).

Pictured on page 53.

# CHOCOLATE SAUERKRAUT CAKE

*Surprise! This actually is a treat to eat. Finely textured.*

| | | |
|---|---|---|
| Butter or margarine, softened | ²/₃ cup | 150 mL |
| Granulated sugar | 1¹/₂ cups | 350 mL |
| Eggs | 3 | 3 |
| Vanilla | 1 tsp. | 5 mL |
| All-purpose flour | 2¹/₄ cups | 500 mL |
| Cocoa | ¹/₂ cup | 125 mL |
| Baking powder | 1 tsp. | 5 mL |
| Baking soda | 1 tsp. | 5 mL |
| Salt | ¹/₂ tsp. | 2 mL |
| Water or prepared coffee | 1 cup | 225 mL |
| Sauerkraut, rinsed, drained, chopped | ²/₃ cup | 150 mL |

Preheat oven to 350°F (180°C). Cream butter well in mixing bowl. Beat in sugar until fluffy. Beat in eggs 1 at a time. Mix in vanilla.

Measure next 5 dry ingredients into small bowl. Stir to mix.

Add flour mixture to butter mixture in 3 parts alternately with water in 2 parts, beginning and ending with flour.

Stir in sauerkraut. Spread in greased 9 × 13 inch (22 × 33 cm) pan or 2 round 8 inch (20 cm) layer pans. Bake in oven for 35 to 40 minutes (25 to 30 minutes for layers) until an inserted wooden pick comes out clean. Ice with Simple Chocolate Icing, page 148.

# MOSAIC CAKE

*So colorful. So rich. So good. So hard to keep on hand.*

| | | |
|---|---|---|
| Butter or margarine, softened | 3 tbsp. | 50 mL |
| Granulated sugar | 1 cup | 250 mL |
| Eggs | 2 | 2 |
| All-purpose flour | 1/2 cup | 125 mL |
| Baking powder | 1/2 tsp. | 2 mL |
| Candied red cherries, halved | 1 cup | 225 mL |
| Candied green cherries, halved | 1 cup | 225 mL |
| Candied pineapple slices, cut up | 3 | 3 |
| Chopped dates | 1 1/2 cups | 350 mL |
| Pecan halves | 3/4 cup | 175 mL |

Preheat oven to 300°F (150°C). Cream butter with sugar in mixing bowl. Beat in eggs 1 at a time.

Stir in flour and baking powder.

Add remaining ingredients. Mix. Line 8 x 8 inch (20 x 20 cm) pan with foil. Turn batter into pan. Bake in oven for about 1 1/2 to 1 3/4 hours until an inserted wooden pick comes out clean. May be served immediately.

# CHERRY CREAM CHEESE CAKE

*This luscious pound cake has a top crust of nuts. Moist and flavorful. Makes a good gift.*

| | | |
|---|---|---|
| Cream cheese, softened | 8 oz. | 250 g |
| Butter or margarine, softened | 1 cup | 250 mL |
| Granulated sugar | 1 1/2 cups | 375 mL |
| Vanilla | 1 1/2 tsp. | 7 mL |
| Eggs | 4 | 4 |
| All-purpose flour | 2 1/4 cups | 550 mL |
| Baking powder | 1 1/2 tsp. | 7 mL |
| Salt | 1/8 tsp. | 0.5 mL |
| Candied cherries, halved (or use maraschino, very well drained) | 1 cup | 250 mL |
| All-purpose flour | 1/4 cup | 50 mL |
| Finely chopped pecans or walnuts | 1/2 cup | 125 mL |

*(continued on next page)*

Preheat oven to 325°F (160°C). Cream the cheese, butter, sugar and vanilla together until smooth.

Beat in eggs 1 at a time.

Combine first amount of flour, baking powder and salt. Fold in.

Stir cherries and second amount of flour together. Add. Fold in.

Sprinkle pecans over bottom of ungreased 10 inch (25 cm) angel food tube pan. Bottom should be completely covered. Add a few more pecans if necessary. Spoon batter into pan. Bake in oven for about 1 hour 15 minutes or until an inserted wooden pick comes out clean. Allow cake to cool. Run knife around outside edge and center tube. Ease out of pan onto plate.

---

# PINEAPPLE CAKE

*Bake this excellent fruity cake one day and serve it any time. It needs no aging. Different from other fruitcakes. Good with or without spice.*

| | | |
|---|---|---|
| Brown sugar, packed | 1 cup | 250 mL |
| Butter or margarine | 1/2 cup | 125 mL |
| Currants | 2 cups | 500 mL |
| Raisins | 1/3 cup | 75 mL |
| Crushed pineapple with juice | 14 oz. | 398 mL |
| Maraschino cherries, chopped | 1/2 cup | 125 mL |
| Eggs, beaten | 2 | 2 |
| All-purpose flour | 2 cups | 450 mL |
| Baking powder | 1 tsp. | 5 mL |
| Salt | 1/2 tsp. | 2 mL |
| Nutmeg | 1 tsp. | 5 mL |
| Mace | 1 tsp. | 5 mL |

Preheat oven to 300°F (150°C). Put first 6 ingredients into large saucepan over medium low heat. Stir often until butter melts. Remove from heat.

Beat eggs until frothy in small bowl. Add to saucepan. Mix well.

Combine remaining ingredients. Add and stir. Pour into foil-lined 8 × 8 inch (20 × 20 cm) pan. Bake in oven for about 1 3/4 hours until an inserted wooden pick comes out clean.

# CHERRY SULTANA CAKE

*A huge cake loaded with raisins. Cherries add some bright spots. No need to wait for it to ripen. This cake can be eaten anytime.*

| | | |
|---|---|---|
| **Raisins** | **4¹/₂ cups** | **1.1 L** |
| **Water to cover** | | |
| | | |
| **Butter or margarine, softened** | **1 cup** | **225 mL** |
| **Granulated sugar** | **1¹/₂ cups** | **350 mL** |
| **Eggs** | **3** | **3** |
| **All-purpose flour** | **3 cups** | **700 mL** |
| **Baking powder** | **1 tbsp.** | **15 mL** |
| **Milk** | **¹/₂ cup** | **125 mL** |
| **Vanilla** | **1 tsp.** | **5 mL** |
| | | |
| **Candied red cherries, halved or quartered** | **1¹/₂ cups** | **375 mL** |

Preheat oven to 325°F (160°C). Cover raisins with water in large saucepan over medium heat. Bring to a boil. Boil 20 minutes. Drain and cool.

In mixing bowl beat next 7 ingredients together well.

Add cherries and raisins. Stir to mix. Scrape into greased and floured 10 inch (25 cm) angel food tube pan or 12 cup (2.7 L) bundt pan. Bake in oven for about 1¹/₂ hours until an inserted wooden pick comes out clean. Needs no icing.

Pictured on page 53.

1. Mocha Chiffon Cake page 28 with Chocolate Mocha Icing page 148
2. Strawberry Shortcake page 112
3. Daffodil Cake page 29 with Lemon Cheese Frosting page 141

# PINEAPPLE UPSIDE DOWN CAKE

*This old timer is always a favorite. Crushed pineapple used in place of sliced is a nice change now and then.*

| | | |
|---|---|---|
| Butter or margarine | 2 tbsp. | 30 mL |
| Pineapple rings | 9 | 9 |
| Maraschino cherries | 9 | 9 |
| Brown sugar, packed | 3/4 cup | 175 mL |
| Butter or margarine, softened | 1/2 cup | 125 mL |
| Granulated sugar | 3/4 cup | 175 mL |
| Eggs, beaten | 2 | 2 |
| Vanilla | 1 tsp. | 5 mL |
| All-purpose flour | 1 1/2 cups | 350 mL |
| Baking powder | 2 tsp. | 10 mL |
| Salt | 1/2 tsp. | 2 mL |
| Milk | 2/3 cup | 150 mL |

Preheat oven to 350°F (180°C). Melt first amount of butter in 9 × 9 inch (22 × 22 cm) pan. Arrange pineapple rings over melted butter. Insert cherries in center of rings. Sprinkle with brown sugar. Set aside.

Cream second amounts of butter and sugar together well in mixing bowl. Add eggs and beat. Mix in vanilla.

Mix flour, baking powder and salt together in small bowl.

Add flour mixture to butter mixture in 3 parts alternately with milk in 2 parts, beginning and ending with flour. Stir after each addition until blended. Pour over top of pineapple. Bake in oven for about 40 to 45 minutes or until an inserted wooden pick comes out clean. Let stand 10 minutes. Loosen edges with knife. Invert onto plate. Cool. Serve with whipped cream.

Pictured on page 35.

**APPLE UPSIDE DOWN CAKE:** Use thinly sliced apples instead of pineapple and cherries. Add a sprinkle of cinnamon.

*Paré Pointer*

*It is really hard to be nostalgic when you can't remember anything.*

# FESTIVE FRUITCAKE

*A large recipe rich and dark enough for any special occasion. Make a few weeks ahead.*

| | | |
|---|---|---|
| Raisins | 4 lbs. | 1.8 kg |
| Currants | 1 lb. | 454 g |
| Candied fruit mix | 2 lbs. | 900 g |
| Candied cherries | 1 lb. | 454 g |
| Jar of maraschino cherries, drained | 16 oz. | 454 g |
| Dates, chopped | 1/2 lb. | 250 g |
| All-purpose flour | 1 cup | 225 mL |
| | | |
| Butter or margarine, softened | 1 lb. | 454 g |
| Granulated sugar | 2 cups | 450 mL |
| Egg yolks | 12 | 12 |
| Crushed pineapple with juice | 14 oz. | 398 mL |
| Vanilla | 1 tbsp. | 15 mL |
| | | |
| All-purpose flour | 2¼ cups | 500 mL |
| Baking powder | 1 tbsp. | 15 mL |
| Baking soda | 1/2 tsp. | 2 mL |
| Salt | 1 tsp. | 5 mL |
| Cocoa | 4 tsp. | 20 mL |
| Cinnamon | 4 tsp. | 20 mL |
| Nutmeg | 2 tsp. | 10 mL |
| | | |
| Fruit juice, such as orange or apple | 1 cup | 225 mL |
| Walnuts, whole or chopped | 1 lb. | 454 g |
| | | |
| Egg whites, room temperature | 12 | 12 |

Preheat oven to 275°F (140°C). First grease four 9 × 5 × 3 inch (23 × 12 × 7 cm) loaf pans. Line with brown paper or foil. Grease again. In large container put first 7 ingredients. Stir to coat with flour.

Cream butter with sugar. Beat in egg yolks, 3 at a time. Stir in pineapple with juice and vanilla.

Measure second amount of flour, baking powder, baking soda, salt, cocoa, cinnamon and nutmeg into bowl. Stir to mix.

Add flour mixture to butter mixture in 3 parts to batter alternately with fruit juice in 2 parts, beginning and ending with flour mixture. Add walnuts.

*(continued on next page)*

Beat egg whites until stiff. Fold into batter. Add fruit. Fold in gently. Divide among pans. Smooth. Bake in oven for about 3 hours until an inserted wooden pick comes out clean. Total weight of 15 lbs. (6.8 kg).

Pictured on page 53.

# DUNDEE CAKE

*A medium colored cake containing a mixture of fruit. A good tea cake.*

| | | |
|---|---|---|
| Raisins | 1 cup | 225 mL |
| Currants | 1 cup | 225 mL |
| Cut mixed peel | 1/3 cup | 75 mL |
| Candied cherries, quartered | 1/3 cup | 75 mL |
| Grated rind of orange | 1 | 1 |
| All-purpose flour | 1/3 cup | 75 mL |
| Butter or margarine, softened | 1 cup | 225 mL |
| Granulated sugar | 1 cup | 225 mL |
| Eggs | 4 | 4 |
| All-purpose flour | 1²/₃ cups | 400 mL |
| Baking powder | 1 tsp. | 5 mL |
| Ground almonds | 2 tbsp. | 30 mL |
| Almonds, split or whole, toasted | 1/2 cup | 125 mL |
| Corn syrup | 1 tbsp. | 15 mL |

Preheat oven to 325°F (160°C). Put first 6 ingredients into bowl. Stir to coat well with flour.

Cream butter and sugar until fluffy. Beat in eggs 1 at a time until light.

Combine remaining flour, baking powder and ground almonds and fold into batter mixture. Add fruit. Mix in. Spread in round foil-lined 8 inch (20 cm) × 3 inch (7.5 cm) deep pan. If using a different size pan fill 3/4 full. Bake in oven for about 1¹/₂ hours until an inserted wooden pick comes out clean. Remove from pan.

Toast almonds in 350°F (180°C) oven until lightly browned, about 5 minutes. Heat corn syrup. Brush over top surface of hot cake. Place almonds in whatever design you like. After cooling, cake will not be sticky. Weighs about 2³/₄ pounds (1.25 kg).

Pictured on page 53.

# BURNT SUGAR CAKE

*A rich caramel flavor all its own. Keep a jar of burnt sugar on hand for convenience. It stores indefinitely.*

| | | |
|---|---|---|
| Butter or margarine, softened | 1/2 cup | 125 mL |
| Granulated sugar | 1 cup | 250 mL |
| Eggs | 2 | 2 |
| Vanilla | 1 tsp. | 5 mL |
| All-purpose flour | 2 cups | 500 mL |
| Baking powder | 2 tsp. | 10 mL |
| Salt | 1/4 tsp. | 1 mL |
| Burnt Sugar Syrup, see page 137 | 1/3 cup | 75 mL |
| Water | 1 cup | 250 mL |

Preheat oven to 350°F (180°C). Cream butter and sugar together well. Beat in eggs 1 at a time. Add vanilla. Stir.

Sift flour, baking powder and salt together.

Mix burnt sugar syrup with water. Add to butter mixture in 2 parts alternately with flour mixture in 3 parts, beginning and ending with flour mixture. Divide batter between 2 greased 8 inch (20 cm) round layer pans. Bake in oven for 30 to 35 minutes until an inserted wooden pick comes out clean. Cool and ice with Burnt Sugar Icing, page 150 or Caramel Icing, page 138.

# ICE CREAM CAKE

*A delight to eat. For a great Banana Split Cake, arrange sliced banana over plate, lay wedge of cake over top and add whipped cream, walnuts and a cherry.*

| | | |
|---|---|---|
| White cake layer, such as Boston Cream Pie, page 118 | 1 | 1 |
| Vanilla ice cream, softened | 2 cups | 500 mL |
| Butterscotch topping | 1/3 cup | 75 mL |
| Strawberry ice cream, softened | 2 cups | 500 mL |
| Strawberry topping | 1/3 cup | 75 mL |
| Chocolate ice cream, softened | 2 cups | 500 mL |
| Chocolate topping | 1/3 cup | 75 mL |
| Whipping cream (or 1 env. topping) | 1 cup | 250 mL |
| Granulated sugar | 1 tbsp. | 15 mL |
| Vanilla | 1/2 tsp. | 2 mL |
| Finely chopped walnuts, sprinkle Maraschino cherries, for garnish | | |

*(continued on next page)*

Bake cake in 8 inch (20 cm) round pan. Slice into 3 layers. Place 1 layer in 8 inch (20 cm) springform pan. Spread with vanilla ice cream. Drizzle with butterscotch topping. Freeze.

Place second layer over top of butterscotch topping. Spread with strawberry ice cream. Drizzle with strawberry topping. Freeze.

Place third cake layer over strawberry topping. Spread with chocolate ice cream. Drizzle with chocolate topping. Freeze.

Beat cream, sugar and vanilla together in mixing bowl until stiff. Cut cake into wedges. Put a wedge on plate. Top with a dollop of whipped cream.

Sprinkle with walnuts, garnish with cherries. If you prefer, spread whipped cream over cake and garnish with walnuts and cherries before cutting.

# BROWN SUGAR POUND CAKE

*This is it. This is that special cake you've been searching for. Nutty and moist. Absolutely incredible in good taste. A large one.*

| | | |
|---|---|---|
| Butter or margarine, softened (butter is best) | 1¹/₂ cups | 350 mL |
| Brown sugar, packed | 4 cups | 900 mL |
| Eggs | 5 | 5 |
| Vanilla | 1 tsp. | 5 mL |
| Maple flavoring | ¹/₂ tsp. | 2 mL |
| All-purpose flour | 3 cups | 700 mL |
| Baking powder | ¹/₂ tsp. | 2 mL |
| Salt | ¹/₂ tsp. | 2 mL |
| Milk | 1 cup | 225 mL |
| Finely chopped pecans or walnuts | 1 cup | 225 mL |

Preheat oven to 325°F (160°C). Cream butter until fluffy. Gradually beat in sugar. Add eggs 1 at a time. Beat well after each addition. Mix in vanilla and maple flavoring.

Measure flour, baking powder and salt into separate bowl. Stir.

Add flour mixture to butter mixture in 3 parts alternately with milk in 2 parts, beginning and ending with flour.

Fold in pecans. Turn into greased and floured 10 inch (25 cm) angel food tube pan. Bake in oven for 1¹/₄ to 1¹/₂ hours until an inserted wooden pick comes out clean.

# RAINBOW CAKE

*All the colors of the rainbow with a fluffy strawberry frosting.*

| | | |
|---|---|---|
| Eggs, room temperature | 4 | 4 |
| Granulated sugar | 1 cup | 225 mL |
| All-purpose flour | 2 cups | 450 mL |
| Baking powder | 2 tsp. | 10 mL |
| Salt | ¼ tsp. | 1 mL |
| Hot milk | 1 cup | 225 mL |
| Butter or margarine | 2 tbsp. | 30 mL |
| Vanilla | 1 tsp. | 5 mL |

**Yellow, red and green food coloring**

Preheat oven to 350°F (180°C). Beat eggs in mixing bowl until frothy. Gradually beat in sugar. Beat until light colored and thick.

Mix flour, baking powder and salt together. Fold into egg mixture.

Into hot milk stir butter and vanilla until melted. Add and fold into batter. Divide batter into 3 equal parts.

**First Layer:** Add a few drops of red food coloring into one batter. Stir to mix. Spread in greased 9 x 9 inch (22 x 22 cm) pan.

**Second Portion:** Add a few drops of yellow food coloring into another batter. Stir to mix. Spread in greased 9 x 9 inch (22 x 22 cm) pan.

**Third Portion:** Add a few drops of green food coloring into remaining batter. Stir to mix. Spread in greased 9 x 9 inch (22 x 22 cm) pan.

Bake in oven for about 10 to 15 minutes until an inserted wooden pick comes out clean. Let stand 8 to 10 minutes. Turn out onto racks to cool.

**FINISHING TOUCHES:**

| | | |
|---|---|---|
| Apple or crabapple jelly | ½ cup | 125 mL |

Trim cake layers of rough edges. Cut each layer into 2 even strips. Mash jelly with fork. Spread some over 1 pink strip on tray. Spread 1 green strip with jelly and place on top. Spread yellow strip with jelly and place on top of green strip. Repeat with remaining 3 strips in same order making 6 layers. Spread jelly on top and sides if preferred but not necessary. Trim edges if needed. Frost with Strawberry Fluff, page 140.

*This requires no icing but one of the suggested icings would compliment it. Delicious flavor.*

| | | |
|---|---|---|
| Butter or margarine, softened | ¹/₂ cup | 125 mL |
| Granulated sugar | 1 cup | 250 mL |
| Eggs | 2 | 2 |
| Maple flavoring | 1 tsp. | 5 mL |
| All-purpose flour | 1¹/₂ cups | 375 mL |
| Baking powder | 2 tsp. | 10 mL |
| Salt | ¹/₄ tsp. | 1 mL |
| Milk | ¹/₂ cup | 125 mL |
| Chopped walnuts | ¹/₂ cup | 125 mL |

Preheat oven to 350°F (180°C). Cream butter well in mixing bowl. Add sugar. Beat until light. Beat in eggs 1 at a time. Add maple flavoring. Stir.

Put flour, baking powder and salt into small bowl. Stir.

Add flour mixture to butter mixture in 3 parts alternately with milk in 2 parts, beginning and ending with flour.

Stir in walnuts. Turn into greased 8 × 8 inch (20 × 20 cm) pan. Bake in oven for about 40 to 45 minutes until an inserted wooden pick comes out clean. Frost with Maple Icing, page 150, Coffee Icing, page 150 or Caramel Icing, page 138.

*They say that money talks. If it could, all it would say is "What happened?"*

# TOLL HOUSE CAKE

*A chocolate chip cake. Good.*

| | | |
|---|---|---|
| Finely chopped walnuts or pecans | ¹/₂ cup | 125 mL |
| Butter or margarine, softened | ³/₄ cup | 175 mL |
| Brown sugar, packed | 1 cup | 225 mL |
| Eggs | 4 | 4 |
| Vanilla | 1¹/₂ tsp. | 7 mL |
| All-purpose flour | 2 cups | 450 mL |
| Baking powder | 1 tbsp. | 15 mL |
| Salt | ¹/₂ tsp. | 2 mL |
| Semisweet chocolate chips | 1¹/₂ cups | 350 mL |

Preheat oven to 350°F (180°C). Sprinkle nuts evenly in bottom of ungreased 8 inch (20 cm) round × 3 inch (7.5 cm) deep pan. Set aside.

Cream butter and sugar together well. Beat in eggs 1 at a time. Stir in vanilla.

Combine flour, baking powder and salt. Add. Stir to moisten.

Fold in chocolate chips. Spoon carefully over nuts in pan. Bake in oven for about 50 to 55 minutes until an inserted wooden pick comes out clean. Let stand 20 minutes. Turn out onto plate or rack.

**Note:** Nuts can be omitted in which case you would grease pan. Cake can be turned right side up. Drizzle outside top edge with melted chocolate, letting it run down the sides a bit. If using a different size pan fill ³/₄ full.

Pictured on page 107.

# BATTENBURG

*A fancy tea cake with a marzipan wrapping.*

| | | |
|---|---|---|
| Butter or margarine, softened | 1 cup | 225 mL |
| Granulated sugar | 1 cup | 225 mL |
| Eggs | 3 | 3 |
| Vanilla | ¹/₄ tsp. | 1 mL |
| All-purpose flour | 2 cups | 450 mL |
| Baking powder | 1 tsp. | 5 mL |
| Salt | ¹/₈ tsp. | 0.5 mL |

*(continued on next page)*

**Red food coloring**

| | | |
|---|---|---|
| **Apricot jam** | **1 cup** | **225 mL** |

**ALMOND PASTE**

| | | |
|---|---|---|
| **Finely ground almonds** | **2 cups** | **450 mL** |
| **Icing (confectioner's) sugar** | **3 cups** | **700 mL** |
| **Egg, room temperature** | **1** | **1** |
| **Lemon juice** | **1¹/₂ tsp.** | **7 mL** |
| **Almond flavoring** | **¹/₄ tsp.** | **1 mL** |

Preheat oven to 350°F (180°C). Cream butter and sugar together. Beat in eggs, 1 at a time. Mix in vanilla.

Add flour, baking powder and salt. Stir gently to mix. If too stiff to be spreadable, add a bit of milk. Divide batter into 2 equal parts.

Add food coloring to 1 part to make a deep pink color.

Grease two 7 × 7 inch (18 × 18 cm) pans. Spread each batter into a pan. Bake in oven until an inserted wooden pick comes out clean, about 25 to 30 minutes. Let stand 5 minutes. Turn out on racks to cool.

Trim edges from both cakes.

Cut each cake lengthwise into 4 strips as wide as the cake is thick. Trim to make strips match. Heat jam slightly. Spread on sides to glue 2 pink and 2 white strips together in checkerboard fashion. Spread all 4 sides of completed cake with jam. Wrap with Almond Paste as follows.

**Almond Paste:** Mix all together. Knead until smooth adding a bit of lemon juice or water if too dry to roll. Add only ¹/₂ tsp. (2 mL) at a time. It will be stiff. Roll ¹/₂ of paste ¹/₈ inch (3 mm) or so thick on lightly icing-sugared surface. Cut to fit length of cake and long enough to cover 4 sides leaving ends uncovered. Lay cake on one end of paste. Wrap to completely enclose all 4 sides of cake pinching paste to seal. Roll in granulated sugar. Place with seal underneath on serving plate or store in plastic bag. Repeat for second cake. Chill. Slice thinly to serve. Makes 2 cakes.

Pictured on page 53.

# POPCORN CAKE

*Just bursting with color. Kids will love it. Best eaten the same day it is made.*

| | | |
|---|---|---|
| Butter or margarine | 1 cup | 250 mL |
| Large marshmallows | 32 | 32 |
| Popped popcorn (pop about ³/₄ cup, 175 mL) | 16 cups | 3.75 L |
| Small gumdrops (no black) | 1 cup | 225 mL |
| Chocolate covered peanuts | 1 cup | 225 mL |
| Smarties or other coated chocolate candy | 1 cup | 225 mL |

Melt butter and marshmallows in large heavy pan over low heat. Stir often.

Put popcorn into large container. Pour marshmallow mixture over top. Stir to mix well.

Add remaining ingredients. Mix together. Pack into greased 10 inch (25 cm) angel food tube pan or 12 cup (2.7 L) bundt pan. Let set until cool. Turn out onto plate to serve. Cut into wedges for all different size kids.

Pictured on page 17.

# NUTTY GRAHAM CAKE

*Exceptionally good. The orange gives this just the right touch.*

| | | |
|---|---|---|
| All-purpose flour | 2 cups | 500 mL |
| Brown sugar, packed | 1¹/₂ cups | 375 mL |
| Graham cracker crumbs | 1 cup | 250 mL |
| Baking powder | 1 tsp. | 5 mL |
| Baking soda | 1 tsp. | 5 mL |
| Salt | 1 tsp. | 5 mL |
| Cinnamon | ¹/₂ tsp. | 2 mL |
| Butter or margarine, softened | 1 cup | 250 mL |
| Prepared orange juice | 1 cup | 250 mL |
| Grated orange rind | 1 tbsp. | 15 mL |
| Eggs | 3 | 3 |
| Chopped walnuts | 1 cup | 250 mL |

*(continued on next page)*

Preheat oven to 350°F (180°C). Measure first 11 ingredients into mixing bowl. Beat until smooth, about 2 to 3 minutes.

Stir in walnuts. Pour into greased and floured 12 cup (2.7 L) bundt pan. Bake in oven for 45 to 50 minutes until an inserted wooden pick comes out clean. Let stand 20 minutes. Invert onto serving plate. Cool. Ice with Brown Sugar Glaze, page 146.

# NUTMEG CAKE

*Very uncommon and very good.*

| | | |
|---|---|---|
| **Eggs** | 3 | 3 |
| **Butter or margarine, softened** | 1/2 cup | 125 mL |
| **Granulated sugar** | 1 1/2 cups | 375 mL |
| **Buttermilk** | 1 cup | 250 mL |
| **Vanilla** | 1 tsp. | 5 mL |
| **All-purpose flour** | 2 cups | 500 mL |
| **Baking powder** | 1 tsp. | 5 mL |
| **Baking soda** | 1 tsp. | 5 mL |
| **Nutmeg** | 2 tsp. | 10 mL |
| **Salt** | 1/4 tsp. | 1 mL |

Preheat oven to 350°F (180°C). Beat eggs well in small bowl.

In mixing bowl cream butter and sugar together well. Add eggs. Beat to mix.

Measure buttermilk. Stir in vanilla.

Combine remaining dry ingredients. Add to butter mixture in 3 parts alternately with buttermilk in 2 parts, beginning and ending with flour mixture. Spread in 2 greased round 9 inch (22 cm) layer pans. Bake in oven for 25 to 30 minutes until an inserted wooden pick comes out clean. Cool. Frost with Caramel Icing, page 138.

**Note:** This may be baked in 9 × 13 inch (22 × 33 cm) pan. Allow about 10 minutes more baking time. Spread topping for Lazy Daisy Cake, page 115, over top and return to oven until bubbly.

# MOCHA CAKE

*Wonderful cake, coffee flavored with coffee filling and icing to match. Definitely a Java connection. Perhaps even Brazil.*

| | | |
|---|---|---|
| Butter or margarine, softened | 1/2 cup | 125 mL |
| Granulated sugar | 1 1/4 cups | 275 mL |
| Eggs, room temperature | 2 | 2 |
| Vanilla | 1 tsp. | 5 mL |
| All-purpose flour | 2 1/4 cups | 525 mL |
| Baking powder | 2 1/4 tsp. | 11 mL |
| Salt | 3/4 tsp. | 4 mL |
| Instant coffee granules | 1 tbsp. | 15 mL |
| Boiling water | 1/4 cup | 60 mL |
| Milk | 1/2 cup | 125 mL |

Preheat oven to 350°F (180°C). Cream butter and sugar together until light and fluffy. Beat in eggs 1 at a time. Mix in vanilla.

Stir flour, baking powder and salt together in small bowl.

Dissolve coffee granules in boiling water. Add to milk. Add flour mixture to butter mixture in 3 parts alternately with milk mixture in 2 parts, beginning and ending with flour. Pour into 2 greased round 8 inch (20 cm) layer pans. Bake in oven for about 30 to 40 minutes until an inserted wooden pick comes out clean. Let stand 10 minutes. Turn out onto racks to cool.

## FILLING

| | | |
|---|---|---|
| Vanilla pudding mix (not instant) 4 serving size | 1 | 1 |
| Instant coffee granules | 1 tbsp. | 15 mL |
| Milk | 1 cup | 225 mL |

Put pudding mix, coffee granules and milk into small saucepan. Mix well. Heat and stir over medium heat until it boils and thickens. Cool thoroughly. It speeds cooling to put saucepan in ice water. Stir often. Spread between cake layers.

## COFFEE FROSTING

| | | |
|---|---|---|
| Butter or margarine, softened (butter is best) | 1 1/2 cups | 350 mL |
| Icing (confectioner's) sugar | 1 1/2 cups | 350 mL |
| Instant coffee granules, powdered | 1 tbsp. | 15 mL |
| Vanilla | 2 tsp. | 10 mL |
| Egg | 1 | 1 |

*(continued on next page)*

Cream butter until fluffy and light. Gradually add icing sugar. Add coffee, vanilla and egg. Beat well. Add water if needed to make proper spreading consistency. Frost sides and top of cake.

## ORANGE CAKE

*A lemony color with a refreshing orange flavor.*

| | | |
|---|---|---|
| **Butter or margarine, softened** | 1/2 cup | 125 mL |
| **Granulated sugar** | 1 1/2 cups | 375 mL |
| **Eggs** | 3 | 3 |
| **Grated orange rind** | 1 tbsp. | 15 mL |
| **All-purpose flour** | 2 cups | 500 mL |
| **Baking powder** | 1 tbsp. | 15 mL |
| **Salt** | 1/2 tsp. | 2 mL |
| **Prepared orange juice** | 1 cup | 250 mL |

Preheat oven to 350°F (180°C). Cream butter and sugar well. Beat in eggs 1 at a time. Add orange rind. Mix.

Combine flour, baking powder and salt in small bowl.

Add orange juice to butter mixture in 2 parts alternately with flour mixture in 3 parts, beginning and ending with flour mixture. Spread in 2 greased 9 inch (22 cm) round layer pans. Bake in oven for 25 to 30 minutes until an inserted wooden pick comes out clean. Ice with Orange Icing, page 150 or Simple Chocolate Icing, page 148.

*She used to have an hourglass shape but time is running out.*

# FRUIT FLAN

*With one of these in the freezer you can feel secure knowing it will thaw quickly. Use any fruit available to fill. Design your own pattern.*

## CAKE

| | | |
|---|---|---|
| All-purpose flour | 1 cup | 250 mL |
| Baking powder | 1¹/₂ tsp. | 7 mL |
| Salt | ¹/₄ tsp. | 1 mL |
| Granulated sugar | ¹/₂ cup | 125 mL |
| Butter or margarine, softened | ¹/₂ cup | 125 mL |
| Eggs, room temperature | 2 | 2 |
| Milk | ¹/₄ cup | 60 mL |

## FILLING

| | | |
|---|---|---|
| Cream cheese, softened | 8 oz. | 250 g |
| Granulated sugar | ¹/₃ cup | 75 mL |
| Lemon juice | 1 tsp. | 5 mL |
| Vanilla | 1 tsp. | 5 mL |

## FRUIT TOPPING
Variety of fruit, fresh, canned or both

## GLAZE

| | | |
|---|---|---|
| Apricot jam or apple jelly | 2 tbsp. | 30 mL |
| Water | 1¹/₂ tsp. | 7 mL |

Preheat oven to 350°F (180°C).

**Cake:** Measure all ingredients into mixing bowl. Mix to moisten. Beat for 2 minutes until smooth. Pour into greased and floured 9¹/₂ inch (24 cm) flan pan. Bake in oven for about 15 to 20 minutes until an inserted wooden pick comes out clean. Let stand for 2 to 3 minutes. Turn out onto rack to cool.

**Filling:** Beat all 4 ingredients together in bowl until smooth. Spread in hollow of flan. Chill to firm a bit.

**Fruit Topping:** Drain fresh or canned fruit very well. Blot with paper towels if necessary. Make a pattern of your choice as you lay the fruit over filling.

**Glaze:** If using apricot jam and water, put through sieve. If using apple jelly and water, melt together then cool. Brush over fruit.

Pictured on page 71.

# PEANUT BUTTER LAYER CAKE

*Such a genuine flavor. Moist and an appetizing color.*

| | | |
|---|---|---|
| Butter or margarine, softened | 1/2 cup | 125 mL |
| Smooth peanut butter | 1/2 cup | 125 mL |
| Brown sugar, packed | 1 1/2 cups | 375 mL |
| Eggs | 2 | 2 |
| Vanilla | 1 tsp. | 5 mL |
| All-purpose flour | 2 cups | 500 mL |
| Baking powder | 2 1/2 tsp. | 12 mL |
| Milk | 1 cup | 250 mL |

Preheat oven to 350°F (180°C). Cream butter and peanut butter together in mixing bowl. Add sugar and beat until fluffy. Beat in eggs 1 at a time. Mix in vanilla.

Stir flour and baking powder together in small bowl.

Add flour to butter mixture in 3 parts alternately with milk in 2 parts, beginning and ending with flour. Pour into 2 greased 8 inch (20 cm) round layer pans. Bake in oven for 30 to 35 minutes until an inserted wooden pick comes out clean.

# BISCUIT SHORTCAKE

*A summertime favorite that is welcome any time of year.*

| | | |
|---|---|---|
| All-purpose flour | 2 1/2 cups | 575 mL |
| Granulated sugar | 1/2 cup | 125 mL |
| Baking powder | 5 tsp. | 25 mL |
| Salt | 1 tsp. | 5 mL |
| Cream of tartar | 1/2 tsp. | 2 mL |
| Butter or margarine, melted | 1/2 cup | 125 mL |
| Milk | 3/4 cup | 175 mL |

Preheat oven to 425°F (220°C). Stir flour, sugar, baking powder, salt and cream of tartar together in bowl.

Add melted butter and milk. Stir to make a soft ball. Press evenly in 2 greased 8 inch (20 cm) round layer pans. Bake in oven for about 12 or 15 minutes until golden brown. Let stand 5 minutes. Turn out onto racks to cool. Finish as for Strawberry Shortcake, page 112.

# CREAM CAKE

*Makes a fast delicate white cake. Heavy cream is used instead of butter.*

| | | |
|---|---|---|
| **Eggs** | 2 | 2 |
| **Granulated sugar** | ³/₄ cup | 175 mL |
| **Vanilla** | 1 tsp. | 5 mL |
| **All-purpose flour** | 1¹/₂ cups | 375 mL |
| **Baking powder** | 2 tsp. | 10 mL |
| **Salt** | 1 tsp. | 5 mL |
| **Whipping cream** | 1 cup | 250 mL |

Preheat oven to 350°F (180°C). Beat eggs in small bowl until very thick. Pour into mixing bowl.

Add sugar and vanilla. Beat well.

Measure flour, baking powder and salt into another bowl. Stir.

Add cream to batter in 2 parts alternately with flour mixture in 3 parts, beginning and ending with dry mixture. Pour into greased 9 × 9 inch (22 × 22 cm) pan. Bake in oven for 30 to 40 minutes until an inserted wooden pick comes out clean.

1. Toll House Cake page 98
2. Pecan Torte with Mocha Cream Filling and Frosting page 61
3. Zucchini Cake page 43 with Cream Cheese Icing page 145
4. Coconut Meringue Cake page 113
5. Mississippi Mud Cake page 76
6. Fruit Cocktail Cake page 129
7. Chocolate Cream Cheese Cake page 68 with Chocolate Cheese Icing page 145
8. Oatmeal Cake with Broiled Topping page 39

*This towering cake is four stories high. The luscious filling is most showy when a slice is placed on a medium size plate.*

| | | |
|---|---|---|
| Butter or margarine, softened | 1 cup | 250 mL |
| Granulated sugar | 2 cups | 500 mL |
| Vanilla | 1 tsp. | 5 mL |
| All-purpose flour | 3¼ cups | 800 mL |
| Baking powder | 1 tbsp. | 15 mL |
| Salt | ¾ tsp. | 4 mL |
| Milk | 1 cup | 250 mL |
| Egg whites, room temperature | 8 | 8 |
| **FILLING** | | |
| Butter or margarine | ½ cup | 125 mL |
| Granulated sugar | 1¼ cups | 300 mL |
| Egg yolks | 8 | 8 |
| Water | ½ cup | 125 mL |
| Brandy flavoring, to taste | 1 tsp. | 5 mL |
| Chopped pecans | 1 cup | 250 mL |
| Raisins | 1 cup | 250 mL |
| Chopped candied cherries | ½ cup | 125 mL |
| Medium coconut | ½ cup | 125 mL |

Preheat oven to 350°F (180°C). Cream butter, sugar and vanilla together in mixing bowl.

Combine flour, baking powder and salt.

Add flour mixture to butter mixture in 3 parts alternately with milk in 2 parts, beginning and ending with flour.

Beat egg whites with clean beaters until stiff. Fold into batter. Spread into 4 greased and floured 8 inch (20 cm) round layer pans. Bake in oven for about 25 minutes or until an inserted wooden pick comes out clean. Cool.

**Filling:** Put butter and sugar into top of double boiler away from heat. Beat together. Add egg yolks and beat well. Stir in water and brandy flavoring. Place over boiling water. Cook and stir until thickened.

Add pecans, raisins, cherries and coconut. Stir. Remove from heat. Cool. Spread between layers. Ice with Seven Minute Frosting, page 147 or Butter Icing, page 150.

# LADY BALTIMORE

*A three layered beauty with a fruity-nutty filling and covered with a soft icing. Not as rich as Lady Baltimore's husband.*

| | | |
|---|---|---|
| Butter or margarine, softened | 1 cup | 250 mL |
| Granulated sugar | 1¼ cup | 300 mL |
| Vanilla | 1½ tsp. | 7 mL |
| All-purpose flour | 3 cups | 750 mL |
| Baking powder | 1 tbsp. | 15 mL |
| Salt | ½ tsp. | 2 mL |
| Milk | 1 cup | 250 mL |
| Egg whites, room temperature | 6 | 6 |
| Granulated sugar | ½ cup | 125 mL |

Preheat oven to 350°F (180°C). Cream butter, first amount of sugar and vanilla together well in mixing bowl. Beat until light and fluffy.

Stir flour, baking powder and salt together in bowl.

Beat flour mixture into margarine mixture in 3 parts alternately with milk in 2 parts, beginning and ending with flour. Batter will be slightly stiff.

Using clean beaters, beat egg whites in mixing bowl until soft peaks form. Add remaining sugar gradually while beating until stiff. Fold into batter. Turn into 3 greased and floured 9 inch (22 cm) round layer pans. Bake in oven for 25 to 30 minutes until an inserted wooden pick comes out clean. Cool assemble with Lady Baltimore Filling and Frosting. A quicker method is to use Seven Minute Frosting, page 147, making an extra recipe for quantity.

## LADY BALTIMORE FROSTING

| | | |
|---|---|---|
| Granulated sugar | 2 cups | 500 mL |
| Water | ⅓ cup | 75 mL |
| Corn syrup | ¼ cup | 60 mL |
| Salt | ⅛ tsp. | 0.5 mL |
| Egg whites, room temperature | 4 | 4 |
| Cream of tartar | ¼ tsp. | 1 mL |
| Sherry (or alcohol-free sherry) or vanilla | 1 tsp. | 5 mL |

In medium saucepan measure in sugar, water, corn syrup and salt over medium heat. Stir to dissolve. Cook to soft ball stage 240°F (115°C) without stirring. It should fall from spoon in a thin thread.

*(continued on next page)*

Beat egg whites and cream of tartar until stiff peaks form shortly before syrup has reached the soft ball stage. When ready, pour syrup in a thin stream over stiff egg whites being careful to beat continuously the whole time. Beat until the right spreading consistency. Measure out 2 cups (500 mL) to use in filling.

**LADY BALTIMORE FILLING**

| | | |
|---|---|---|
| **Reserved frosting** | **2 cups** | **500 mL** |
| **Raisins, coarsely chopped** | **½ cup** | **125 mL** |
| **Chopped pecans or walnuts** | **⅓ cup** | **75 mL** |
| **Candied cherries, cut up** | **⅓ cup** | **75 mL** |
| **Sherry (or alcohol-free sherry)** | **2 tsp.** | **10 mL** |

Stir all together. Use to spread between layers. Coat the top and sides of cake with remaining frosting.

# ONE BOWL WHITE CAKE

*So simple. Just measure everything into one bowl and beat.*

| | | |
|---|---|---|
| **All-purpose flour** | **2 cups** | **500 mL** |
| **Baking powder** | **2 tsp.** | **10 mL** |
| **Salt** | **½ tsp.** | **2 mL** |
| **Granulated sugar** | **1 cup** | **250 mL** |
| **Butter or margarine, softened** | **½ cup** | **125 mL** |
| **Eggs** | **2** | **2** |
| **Vanilla** | **1 tsp.** | **5 mL** |
| **Milk** | **1 cup** | **250 mL** |

Preheat oven to 350°F (180°C). Put all ingredients into mixing bowl. Beat slowly to moisten then beat at medium speed until smooth, about 2 minutes. Pour into 2 greased 8 or 9 inch (20 or 22 cm) round layer pans. Bake in oven until an inserted wooden pick comes out clean, about 30 to 35 minutes.

**Note:** For a quick family cake, bake in 9 x 9 inch (22 x 22 cm) pan. Cool and frost.

**MARBLE CAKE:** Reserve ¾ cup (175 mL) batter. Stir in 2 tbsp. (30 mL) cocoa. Drop by spoonfuls over top. Use cutting motion with knife to swirl.

# STRAWBERRY SHORTCAKE

*A family favorite from awa-a-ay back that is welcome anytime.*

| | | |
|---|---|---|
| Baked 2 layer cake, yellow or white, your own or a mix, see page 111. If you prefer a biscuit shortcake, see page 105. | 1 | 1 |
| Fresh strawberries, cut and mashed | 4 cups | 1 L |
| Granulated sugar, to taste | 2-4 tbsp. | 30-60 mL |
| Whipping cream (or 1 envelope topping) | 1 cup | 250 mL |
| Granulated sugar | 1 tbsp. | 15 mL |
| Vanilla | 1/2 tsp. | 2 mL |

Place 1 cake layer rounded side down on serving plate.

Mash berries and first amount of sugar together. This is easier to do 1/2 at a time. Put 1/2 berries and juice over cake on plate. Place second layer of cake on top rounded side up. Spoon second 1/2 berries and juice over top. Allow a bit of juice to run down sides. If top of cake is peaked, trim to flatten so berries stay on.

Whip cream, remaining sugar and vanilla together in small mixing bowl until stiff. Spoon on top. Yumm!

**Garnish:** Dip a few whole strawberries into melted white or semisweet chocolate. Arrange around cake.

Pictured on page 89.

*When a goose wants to find a boyfriend, she takes a gander.*

# COCONUT MERINGUE CAKE

*This self-iced cake has a thin topping of a coconut-meringue mixture. No further icing needed.*

| | | |
|---|---|---|
| **Butter or margarine, softened** | 1/2 cup | 125 mL |
| **Granulated sugar** | 1/2 cup | 125 mL |
| **Egg yolks** | 3 | 3 |
| **All-purpose flour** | 1 cup | 250 mL |
| **Baking powder** | 11/2 tsp. | 7 mL |
| **Salt** | 1/4 tsp. | 1 mL |
| **Milk** | 1/3 cup | 75 mL |
| **Vanilla** | 1 tsp. | 5 mL |
| **TOPPING** | | |
| **Egg whites, room temperature** | 3 | 3 |
| **Granulated sugar** | 1/2 cup | 125 mL |
| **Medium coconut** | 11/2 cups | 350 mL |

Preheat oven to 350°F (180°C). Cream butter, sugar and egg yolks together in mixing bowl until fluffy.

Combine flour, baking powder and salt in bowl.

Add flour mixture to butter mixture in 2 parts alternately with milk and vanilla in 1 part, beginning and ending with flour mixture. Spread in greased 9 × 9 inch (22 × 22 cm) pan.

**Topping:** Beat egg whites until soft peaks form. Add sugar gradually while beating until stiff.

Fold in coconut. Put spoonfuls here and there over batter. Smooth as best you can. Bake in oven for 30 to 35 minutes until an inserted wooden pick comes out clean.

**Variation:** Brown sugar may be used in the topping as well as in the cake if desired. Flavor is very similar but the color is darker.

Pictured on page 107.

# WHITE CHOCOLATE CAKE

*A lovely delicate flavored cake. It has a moist pound cake texture.*

| | | |
|---|---|---|
| Butter or margarine, softened | 1 cup | 250 mL |
| Granulated sugar | 2 cups | 500 mL |
| Egg yolks, room temperature | 4 | 4 |
| Vanilla | 1 tsp. | 5 mL |
| White baking chocolate squares, melted | 4 × 1 oz. | 4 × 28 g |
| Sifted cake flour | 2¹/₂ cups | 625 mL |
| Baking powder | 1 tsp. | 5 mL |
| Buttermilk | 1 cup | 250 mL |
| Egg whites, room temperature | 4 | 4 |

Preheat oven to 350°F (180°C). Cream butter and sugar together in mixing bowl. Beat in egg yolks. Add vanilla and melted chocolate. Mix.

Sift cake flour and baking powder onto plate.

Add buttermilk to butter mixture in 2 parts alternately with flour in 3 parts, beginning and ending with flour.

Beat egg whites until stiff. Fold into batter. Spread in greased 10 inch (25 cm) angel food tube pan. Bake in oven for 50 to 55 minutes until an inserted wooden pick comes out clean. Cool and ice with White Chocolate Icing, page 138.

# GOLD CAKE

*If you have made or are about to make a cake with a lot of egg whites, this is a recipe to use the leftover yolks. Layers are deep enough to slice to make a four layer cake.*

| | | |
|---|---|---|
| Butter or margarine, softened | ³/₄ cup | 175 mL |
| Granulated sugar | 1¹/₂ cups | 350 mL |
| Egg yolks, room temperature (about 12) | 1 cup | 225 mL |
| Vanilla | 1 tsp. | 5 mL |
| All-purpose flour | 1³/₄ cups | 400 mL |
| Baking powder | 2 tsp. | 10 mL |
| Salt | ¹/₂ tsp. | 2 mL |
| Milk | ³/₄ cup | 175 mL |

*(continued on next page)*

Preheat oven to 350°F (180°C). Cream butter and sugar well in mixing bowl. Beat in egg yolks and vanilla. Beat until fluffy.

Measure flour, baking powder and salt into small bowl. Stir.

Add milk to butter mixture in 2 parts alternately with flour mixture in 3 parts, beginning and ending with flour mixture. Spread in 2 greased 8 inch (20 cm) round layer pans. Bake in oven for about 25 to 30 minutes until an inserted wooden pick comes out clean. Ice with Snow White Icing, page 148, Coffee Icing, page 150 or Simple Chocolate Icing, page 148.

## LAZY DAISY CAKE

*A quick hot milk sponge cake that is good warm or cold. Without the topping it makes a good shortcake that doesn't crumble.*

| | | |
|---|---|---|
| Eggs | 2 | 2 |
| Granulated sugar | 1 cup | 250 mL |
| Vanilla | 1 tsp. | 5 mL |
| All-purpose flour | 1 cup | 250 mL |
| Baking powder | 1 tsp. | 5 mL |
| Salt | 1/2 tsp. | 2 mL |
| Milk | 1/2 cup | 125 mL |
| Butter or margarine | 1 tbsp. | 15 mL |
| TOPPING | | |
| Butter or margarine | 3 tbsp. | 50 mL |
| Brown sugar, packed | 1/2 cup | 125 mL |
| Cream or milk | 2 tbsp. | 30 mL |
| Coconut | 1/2 cup | 125 mL |

Preheat oven to 350°F (180°C). Beat eggs in mixing bowl until frothy. Add sugar gradually while beating until thick. Add vanilla.

Combine flour, baking powder and salt. Stir into egg mixture.

In small saucepan heat milk and butter until hot. Stir into batter. Spread in greased 9 × 9 inch (22 × 22 cm) pan. Bake in oven for 25 to 30 minutes until an inserted wooden pick comes out clean. Cover with topping.

**Topping:** Combine all 4 ingredients together in small saucepan. Heat to melt butter and dissolve sugar. Do not boil. Spread over cake. Return to oven until it bubbles all over the top, about 3 minutes.

# CONE CUPCAKES

*Please a child as well as an adult. Make some cones and some Butterfly Cupcakes.*

| | | |
|---|---|---|
| Butter or margarine, softened | 1/2 cup | 125 mL |
| Granulated sugar | 1 cup | 225 mL |
| Eggs | 2 | 2 |
| Vanilla | 1 tsp. | 5 mL |
| All-purpose flour | 1 3/4 cups | 400 mL |
| Baking powder | 2 1/2 tsp. | 12 mL |
| Salt | 1/4 tsp. | 1 mL |
| Milk | 2/3 cup | 175 mL |
| Flat bottomed ice cream cones | 24 | 24 |

Preheat oven to 375°F (190°C). Cream butter and sugar together well in mixing bowl. Beat in eggs 1 at a time. Mix in vanilla.

Measure flour, baking powder and salt into small bowl. Stir.

Add milk to butter mixture in 2 parts alternately with flour mixture in 3 parts, beginning and ending with flour. Fill cones about 3/4 full leaving the batter 1/2 inch (1 cm) from top. Place filled cones on a baking tray. Bake in oven for about 15 to 20 minutes until an inserted wooden pick comes out clean. Choose whatever color icing you prefer, then decorate if desired. Makes about 24.

Pictured on page 17 using Lemon Icing, page 150, Green Butter Icing, page 150 and Peanut Butter Icing, page 141.

**BUTTERFLY CUPCAKES:** Fill cupcake papers 2/3 full to bake in muffin pan. Bake in 350°F (180°C) oven for about 20 minutes until an inserted wooden pick comes out clean. Cool. Using sharp paring knife, cut a large cone shaped piece from center of each cupcake. Cut in from outside edge about 1/2 inch (12 mm). Fill hollow generously with Lemon Filling, page 136 or filling of your choice. Cut removed cone in half. Place sides that would fit in center of cupcake down on filling to form a butterfly.

**TWINKIE TYPE CUPCAKES:** Bake in cupcake papers in muffin pan. Cool. Make Custard Filling, page 104. Cool filling. Insert pastry tube filled with custard into center of cupcakes and slowly squeeze in filling. Ice with Butter Icing, page 150 or Simple Chocolate Icing, page 148.

*(continued on next page)*

**CHOCOLATE CUPCAKES:** Add 2 tbsp. (30 mL) cocoa to mixture and 1 tbsp. (15 mL) milk.

**CREAM CUPCAKES:** Slice tops off white or chocolate cupcakes. Put on a dollop of whipped cream or some filling from Boston Cream Pie, page 118. Put top back on pressing lightly. Sift icing (confectioner's) sugar over top.

# OLD TIME POUND CAKE

*The original recipe calls for one pound each of all the main ingredients. This is a large cake, a special cake.*

| | | |
|---|---|---|
| Egg whites, room temperature | 10 | 10 |
| Butter or margarine, softened | 2 cups | 450 mL |
| Granulated sugar | 2 cups | 450 mL |
| Egg yolks, beaten | 10 | 10 |
| Baking soda | 1/2 tsp. | 2 mL |
| Water | 1 tsp. | 5 mL |
| Lemon flavoring | 1 tsp. | 5 mL |
| All-purpose flour | 4 cups | 900 mL |
| Cream of tartar | 1 tsp. | 5 mL |

Preheat oven to 300°F (150°C). Beat egg whites in large bowl until stiff. Set aside.

Using same beaters, cream butter and sugar together well in mixing bowl.

Add egg yolks. Beat well. Fold in egg whites.

Dissolve baking soda in water and add lemon flavoring. Fold in.

Combine flour and cream of tartar. Stir. Sift over batter 1/2 at a time. Fold in. Turn into foil-lined 10 inch (25 cm) round × 3 1/2 inch (9 cm) deep pan. If using a different size pan fill 3/4 full. Bake in oven for about 2 hours until an inserted wooden pick comes out clean. Cut into slices rather than wedges to serve.

# BOSTON CREAM PIE

*A simple cake made elegant by the finishing touches of a custard filling and chocolate glaze.*

| | | |
|---|---|---|
| Eggs | 2 | 2 |
| Granulated sugar | ³/₄ cup | 175 mL |
| Butter or margarine, softened | ¹/₃ cup | 75 mL |
| Vanilla | ¹/₂ tsp. | 2 mL |
| All-purpose flour | 1 cup | 225 mL |
| Baking powder | 1 tsp. | 5 mL |
| Salt | ¹/₄ tsp. | 1 mL |
| Milk | ¹/₃ cup | 75 mL |

Preheat oven to 350°F (180°C). Beat eggs in mixing bowl until thick. Beat in sugar, butter and vanilla.

Add flour, baking powder and salt. Stir.

Add milk. Stir and pour into 1 greased 8 inch (20 cm) round layer pan. Bake in oven for about 25 to 30 minutes until an inserted wooden pick comes out clean. Cool. Cut cake to make 2 layers. Spread Custard Filling between layers.

## CUSTARD FILLING

| | | |
|---|---|---|
| Milk | 1 cup | 225 mL |
| Granulated sugar | ¹/₄ cup | 60 mL |
| All-purpose flour | ¹/₄ cup | 60 mL |
| Salt | ¹/₈ tsp. | 0.5 mL |
| Egg | 1 | 1 |
| Vanilla | ¹/₂ tsp. | 2 mL |

Bring milk to a boil in medium saucepan.

Meanwhile mix sugar, flour and salt together thoroughly. Add egg and vanilla. Mix well. Stir into boiling milk to thicken. Remove from heat. Cool. Setting pan in ice water helps to cool quicker. Stir often. Spread between layers. Apply Chocolate Glaze.

## CHOCOLATE GLAZE

| | | |
|---|---|---|
| Icing (confectioner's) sugar | 1 cup | 250 mL |
| Cocoa | 2 tbsp. | 30 mL |
| Butter or margarine, softened | 1 tbsp. | 15 mL |
| Water or milk | 4 tsp. | 20 mL |

*(continued on next page)*

118

Beat all 4 ingredients together in small bowl. Add more water if needed to make a barely pourable glaze. Spread over top of cake. Allow some to drizzle down sides a bit. Chill. Serve with or without whipped cream.

**Note:** A regular 2 layer cake may be used, your own or a mix. Being larger it will give more cake per serving.

# ITALIAN CREAM CAKE

*Makes a large good three layer cake.*

| | | |
|---|---|---|
| Egg whites, room temperature | 5 | 5 |
| Butter or margarine, softened | 1 cup | 250 mL |
| Granulated sugar | 2 cups | 500 mL |
| Egg yolks, room temperature | 5 | 5 |
| Vanilla | 1 tsp. | 5 mL |
| All-purpose flour | 2 cups | 500 mL |
| Salt | 1/2 tsp. | 2 mL |
| Baking soda | 1 tsp. | 5 mL |
| Buttermilk | 1 cup | 250 mL |
| Flaked coconut | 1 cup | 250 mL |

Preheat oven to 350°F (180°C). Beat egg whites until stiff. Set aside.

Cream butter and sugar well. Beat in egg yolks and vanilla until fluffy.

Stir flour and salt together in small bowl.

Stir baking soda into buttermilk. Add flour mixture to egg yolk mixture in 3 parts alternately with buttermilk in 2 parts, beginning and ending with flour mixture.

Fold in coconut. Fold beaten egg whites into batter. Spread in 3 round greased 8 or 9 inch (20 or 22 cm) layer pans. Bake in oven for about 25 to 30 minutes until an inserted wooden pick comes out clean. Cool and frost with Cheese Pecan Frosting, page 145.

# CHOCOLATE CHIP CAKE

*Sour cream, rum flavoring and chocolate chips help to give this its delicious flavor.*

| | | |
|---|---|---|
| Chocolate cake mix, 2 layer size | 1 | 1 |
| Instant chocolate pudding mix, 4 serving size | 1 | 1 |
| Sour cream | 1 cup | 225 mL |
| Cooking oil | 1/2 cup | 125 mL |
| Eggs | 4 | 4 |
| Vanilla | 1 tsp. | 5 mL |
| Rum flavoring | 2 tsp. | 10 mL |
| Semisweet chocolate chips | 1 cup | 250 mL |

Preheat oven to 350°F (180°C). Put first 7 ingredients into mixing bowl. Beat slowly until moistened. Beat at medium speed for 2 minutes.

Fold in chocolate chips. Pour into greased and floured 12 cup (2.7 L) bundt pan. Bake in oven for 50 to 55 minutes until an inserted wooden pick comes out clean. Let stand for 25 minutes. Turn out onto plate to finish cooling. Coat with Chocolate Rum Glaze, page 146.

# SHERRY CAKE

*Moist with a hint of nutmeg. Nice flavor.*

| | | |
|---|---|---|
| Yellow cake mix, 2 layer size | 1 | 1 |
| Instant vanilla pudding mix, 4 serving size | 1 | 1 |
| Cream sherry (or alcohol-free sherry) | 3/4 cup | 175 mL |
| Cooking oil | 3/4 cup | 175 mL |
| Eggs | 4 | 4 |
| Nutmeg | 1 tsp. | 5 mL |

Preheat oven to 350°F (180°C). Measure all ingredients into mixing bowl. Beat slowly to blend. Beat for 2 minutes at medium speed. Turn into greased and floured 12 cup (2.7 L) bundt pan. Bake in oven until an inserted wooden pick comes out clean, about 45 to 50 minutes. Let stand 20 minutes. Turn out onto plate. Cool. Glaze.

**SHERRY GLAZE:** To 1 cup (250 mL) icing (confectioner's) sugar mix in equal amounts of sherry and milk to make a barely pourable glaze. Drizzle over cake.

# CHERRY CHOCOLATE CAKE

*A very easy way to get the good mixture of cherries and chocolate. Moist.*

| | | |
|---|---|---|
| Dark chocolate cake mix, 2 layer size | 1 | 1 |
| Eggs | 3 | 3 |
| Cherry pie filling | 19 oz. | 540 g |
| Almond flavoring | 2 tsp. | 10 mL |

Preheat oven to 350°F (180°C). Combine all ingredients in mixing bowl. Beat until smooth. Turn batter into greased and floured 12 cup (2.7 L) bundt pan or 9 × 13 inch (22 × 33 cm) pan. Bake in oven until an inserted wooden pick comes out clean, about 50 to 55 minutes. Check for doneness sooner in flat pan. Spread with glaze. Serve warm or cold.

**CHOCOLATE CHIP GLAZE**

| | | |
|---|---|---|
| Semisweet chocolate chips | ¹/₂ cup | 125 mL |
| Butter or margarine | 1 tbsp. | 15 mL |
| Milk | 2 tbsp. | 30 mL |
| Icing (confectioner's) sugar | ¹/₂ cup | 125 mL |

Heat chocolate chips, butter and milk in small saucepan over medium heat. Stir often until chips are melted. Remove from heat.

Stir in icing sugar. Spread over cake.

# PEANUT BUTTER CAKE

*A fast way to change a plain cake to suit kids of all ages. Mild flavor.*

| | | |
|---|---|---|
| Yellow cake mix, 2 layer size | 1 | 1 |
| Milk | 1¹/₄ cups | 275 mL |
| Eggs | 3 | 3 |
| Smooth peanut butter | ¹/₂ cup | 125 mL |

Preheat oven to 350°F (180°C). Mix all together until moistened. Beat at medium speed until smooth, about 2 minutes. Turn into greased and floured 12 cup (2.7 L) bundt pan. Bake in oven for 45 to 50 minutes until an inserted wooden pick comes out clean. Let stand 30 minutes. Turn out onto plate. Glaze with Orange Glaze, page 146 or Peanut Butter Icing, page 141.

# PUMPKIN CAKE

*Spicy and moist. An easy pumpkin cake.*

| | | |
|---|---|---|
| Spice cake mix, 2 layer size | 1 | 1 |
| Instant vanilla pudding mix, 4 serving size | 1 | 1 |
| Cooking oil | 1/3 cup | 75 mL |
| Canned pumpkin (without spices) | 1 cup | 225 mL |
| Water | 1/2 cup | 125 mL |
| Eggs | 4 | 4 |
| Cinnamon | 1 tsp. | 5 mL |

Preheat oven to 350°F (180°C). Combine all ingredients to moisten. Beat at medium speed until smooth, about 2 minutes. Turn into greased 9 × 13 inch (22 × 33 cm) pan. Bake in oven until an inserted wooden pick comes out clean, about 40 minutes. Cool. Ice with Cream Cheese Icing, page 145.

# MERINGUE SWIRL

*A very pretty effect is achieved by the swirling of meringue into the top of the unbaked cake. No icing required. A nice browned swirl is the topping.*

| | | |
|---|---|---|
| Egg whites, room temperature | 2 | 2 |
| Salt | 1/4 tsp. | 1 mL |
| Cream of tartar | 1/4 tsp. | 1 mL |
| Granulated sugar | 1/4 cup | 60 mL |
| White or yellow cake mix, 2 layer size | 1 | 1 |

Preheat oven to 350°F (180°C). Beat egg whites, salt and cream of tartar together until stiff.

Add sugar gradually, beating continually until stiff. Set aside.

Using same beaters, prepare cake mix according to package directions. Turn into greased 9 × 13 inch (22 × 33 cm) pan. Put dabs of meringue here and there over top. Spread, swirling lightly into cake batter. Bake in oven for 35 to 40 minutes or until an inserted wooden pick comes out clean.

**Variation:** Use chocolate cake mix. Use brown sugar rather than granulated. Add 1/4 tsp. almond flavoring.

# ORANGE REFRESHMENT CAKE

*Serve this cooler to company on a hot day and see how well it goes over. Refreshing is the word.*

| | | |
|---|---|---|
| Orange flavored gelatin | 3 oz. | 85 g |
| Boiling water | ³/₄ cup | 175 mL |
| Cold water | ¹/₂ cup | 125 mL |
| White cake mix, 2 layer size<br>(not yellow) | 1 | 1 |
| **TOPPING** | | |
| Envelope of dessert topping mix | 1 | 1 |
| Instant vanilla pudding mix,<br>4 serving size | 1 | 1 |
| Cold milk | 1¹/₂ cups | 350 mL |
| Vanilla | 1 tsp. | 5 mL |

Preheat oven to 350°F (180°C). Dissolve orange gelatin in boiling water in small bowl. Add cold water. Set aside on counter. Do not chill.

Prepare cake batter according to package directions. Spread in greased 9 × 13 inch (22 × 33 cm) pan. Bake in oven 35 to 45 minutes until an inserted wooden pick comes out clean. Cool 20 to 25 minutes. With meat fork, poke deep holes right to the bottom about 1 inch (2.5 cm) apart. Put gelatin into small pitcher so it pours easily. Pour into holes in cake. Chill while preparing topping.

**Topping:** Put all ingredients into small mixing bowl. Beat until stiff. Spread over cake. Refrigerate.

**HOLIDAY CAKE:** Use lime flavored gelatin for St. Patrick's Day. May also be baked in two layers. Pour red gelatin over one layer and green over the other. Ready for Christmas. For layers use only 1 cup (250 mL) water with gelatin powder and make holes a bit closer together.

*Crowded colleges usually empty by degrees.*

# CARROT CAKE

*A light and quick carrot cake.*

| | | |
|---|---|---|
| Grated carrots | 1¹/₂ cups | 375 mL |
| Raisins, chopped a bit | ¹/₂ cup | 125 mL |
| All-purpose flour | 2 tbsp. | 30 mL |
| Yellow cake mix, 2 layer size | 1 | 1 |
| Cooking oil | ¹/₃ cup | 75 mL |
| Water | ¹/₃ cup | 75 mL |
| Eggs | 4 | 4 |
| Instant vanilla pudding mix, 4 serving size | 1 | 1 |
| Cinnamon | 2 tsp. | 10 mL |

Preheat oven to 350°F (180°C). Mix carrot and raisins with flour in small bowl.

Put remaining ingredients into mixing bowl. Mix slowly to blend together. Beat at medium speed for 2 minutes until smooth. Fold in carrot-raisin mixture. Turn into greased 9 × 13 inch (22 × 33 cm) pan. Bake in oven until an inserted wooden pick comes out clean, about 45 minutes. Cool. Spread with Cream Cheese Icing, page 145.

Pictured on page 125.

1. Chip and Date Cake page 67
2. Queen Elizabeth Cake with Coconut Topping page 19
3. Poppy Seed Chiffon page 23 with Caramel Icing page 138
4. Peanut Butter Marble Cake page 128 with Vanilla Glaze page 146
5. Matrimonial Cake page 14
6. Tomato Soup Cake page 42 with Simple Chocolate Icing page 148
7. Carrot Cake page 44 with Cream Cheese Icing page 145

The china in this picture belongs to Mrs. Ruby Elford, mother of Jean Paré.

# POPPY SEED CAKE

*No pre-soaking of poppy seeds required for this cake. The lemon cake mix may be exchanged for white or yellow.*

| | | |
|---|---|---|
| Lemon cake mix, 2 layer size | 1 | 1 |
| Instant vanilla pudding mix, 4 serving size | 1 | 1 |
| Cooking oil | 1/2 cup | 125 mL |
| Eggs | 4 | 4 |
| Water | 1 cup | 225 mL |
| Poppy seeds | 1/4 cup | 60 mL |

Preheat oven to 350°F (180°C). Put all ingredients into mixing bowl. Beat slowly to moisten. Beat on medium speed for 2 minutes. Pour into greased and floured 12 cup (2.7 L) bundt pan. Bake in oven for 45 to 55 minutes until an inserted wooden pick comes out clean. Let stand 20 minutes. Invert and turn out onto plate. Cool. Glaze with Maple Icing, page 150, Brown Sugar Glaze, page 146 or Caramel Icing, page 138.

# HARVEY WALLBANGER CAKE

*Not much of a fix when you fix this cake. The alcohol bakes out of course but the flavor and moistness remain.*

| | | |
|---|---|---|
| Yellow cake mix, 2 layer size | 1 | 1 |
| Instant vanilla pudding mix, 4 serving size | 1 | 1 |
| Prepared orange juice | 2/3 cup | 150 mL |
| Vodka | 1/4 cup | 60 mL |
| Galliano liqueur | 1/4 cup | 60 mL |
| Cooking oil | 1/2 cup | 125 mL |
| Eggs | 4 | 4 |

Preheat oven to 350°F (180°C). Put all ingredients into mixing bowl. Blend together to moisten. Beat at medium speed until smooth, about 2 minutes. Turn into 12 cup (2.7 L) greased and floured bundt pan. Bake in oven until an inserted wooden pick comes out clean, about 45 minutes. Let stand 15 to 30 minutes. Remove from pan onto plate. Cool. Dust with icing (confectioner's) sugar or drizzle with Orange Glaze, page 146.

# PEANUT BUTTER MARBLE CAKE

*Looks like a regular marble cake. Flavor is excellent.*

| | | |
|---|---|---|
| Marble cake mix, 2 layer size | 1 | 1 |
| Water | 1 cup | 250 mL |
| Smooth peanut butter | 1/3 cup | 75 mL |
| Cooking oil | 1/4 cup | 60 mL |
| Eggs | 3 | 3 |

**Chocolate envelope from cake mix**

Preheat oven to 350°F (180°C). Put contents of white cake mix pouch, water, peanut butter, cooking oil and eggs into mixing bowl. Mix to moisten. Beat on medium speed 2 minutes until smooth. Put 3/4 of the batter into greased and floured 12 cup (2.7 L) bundt pan.

Add chocolate envelope contents to remaining 1/4 batter. Mix. Spoon over white batter. Using a knife, cut into batter using a swirling motion to marble the batter. Bake in oven for 45 to 50 minutes until an inserted wooden pick comes out clean. Cool 20 to 30 minutes. Invert onto plate. Choco Peanut Glaze, page 145 is good on this cake as is Vanilla Glaze, page 146.

Pictured with Vanilla Glaze on page 125.

# BURNT SUGAR CAKE

*An easy method to get the wonderful flavor of burnt sugar.*

| | | |
|---|---|---|
| White cake mix, 2 layer size | 1 | 1 |
| Instant butterscotch pudding mix, 4 serving size | 1 | 1 |
| Cooking oil | 1/2 cup | 125 mL |
| Burnt Sugar Syrup, see page 137 | 1/4 cup | 50 mL |
| Water | 3/4 cup | 175 mL |
| Eggs | 4 | 4 |

Preheat oven to 350°F (180°C). In large mixing bowl combine cake mix, pudding mix, cooking oil, burnt sugar syrup, water and eggs. Beat slowly to moisten. Beat for 2 minutes until smooth. Turn into greased and floured 12 cup (2.7 L) bundt pan. Bake in oven for about 45 to 50 minutes until an inserted wooden pick comes out clean. Let stand for 20 minutes. Turn out onto plate or rack. Cool. Drizzle with Brown Sugar Glaze, page 146.

# FRUIT COCKTAIL CAKE

*A moist cake that is glazed upon removal from the oven. No further Icing required.*

| | | |
|---|---|---|
| Yellow cake mix, 2 layer size | 1 | 1 |
| Instant lemon pudding mix, 4 serving size | 1 | 1 |
| Flaked coconut | 1 cup | 225 mL |
| Cooking oil | 1/4 cup | 60 mL |
| Eggs | 4 | 4 |
| Fruit cocktail with juice | 14 oz. | 398 mL |
| Brown sugar, packed | 1/2 cup | 125 mL |
| Chopped pecans or walnuts | 1/2 cup | 125 mL |
| **GLAZE** | | |
| Butter or margarine | 1/2 cup | 125 mL |
| Granulated sugar | 1/2 cup | 125 mL |
| Evaporated milk | 1/2 cup | 125 mL |
| Coconut, flaked or medium | 1 cup | 250 mL |

Preheat oven to 325°F (160°C). Put cake mix, pudding mix, coconut, cooking oil, eggs, fruit cocktail and juice into mixing bowl. Beat about 3 minutes. Turn into bottom-greased 9 × 13 inch (22 × 33 cm) pan.

Mix sugar and pecans together. Sprinkle over top. Bake in oven for about 45 to 50 minutes, until an inserted wooden pick comes out clean.

**Glaze:** Put butter, sugar and milk in small saucepan over medium heat. Bring to a boil. Boil 2 minutes.

Stir in coconut. Pour over hot cake.

Pictured on page 107.

*A robot's favorite snack is nuts and bolts.*

# PINEAPPLE UPSIDE DOWN CAKE

*As pretty as a picture. This old favorite feeds the eye to begin with.*

| | | |
|---|---|---|
| Butter or margarine | ¼ cup | 60 mL |
| Brown sugar, packed | 1 cup | 250 mL |
| Canned sliced pineapple rings | 12 | 12 |
| Yellow cake mix, 2 layer size, with pudding added | 1 | 1 |
| Whipping cream (or 1 envelope topping) | 1 cup | 250 mL |
| Granulated sugar | 1 tbsp. | 15 mL |
| Vanilla | ½ tsp. | 2 mL |

Preheat oven to 350°F (180°C). Put butter into 9 x 13 inch (22 x 33 cm) pan. Put in oven to melt. Spread over entire bottom. Sprinkle evenly with sugar. Lay pineapple rings over top.

Mix cake according to package directions. Pour over pineapple. Bake in oven until an inserted wooden pick comes out clean, about 35 minutes. Let stand 5 minutes. Invert onto tray.

Beat cream, sugar vanilla together in bowl until stiff. Serve warm or cold with a dollop of whipped cream on top.

Pictured on page 35.

**Variation:** After laying pineapple in pan, place a maraschino cherry in center of each ring. It adds more expense to the cake but also adds color.

**Variation:** Crushed pineapple, drained, in place of rings makes a very easy to eat cake. Use 2 x 14 oz. (2 x 398 mL) cans.

**FRUITED UPSIDE DOWN CAKE:** Use canned apricots or peaches, drained, in place of pineapple. Sprinkle fruit with chopped nuts as another variation.

*How many blisters do you have to put up with for a place in the sun?*

*Dark and moist with a self iced top crust of nuts.*

| | | |
|---|---|---|
| Chocolate cake mix, 2 layer size | 1 | 1 |
| Instant vanilla pudding mix, 4 serving size | 1 | 1 |
| Cooking oil | 1/2 cup | 125 mL |
| Water | 1/2 cup | 125 mL |
| Rum, light or dark (or 1 tbsp., 15 mL, rum flavoring, plus water) | 1/2 cup | 125 mL |
| Eggs | 4 | 4 |
| Finely chopped pecans or walnuts | 1/2 cup | 125 mL |

Preheat oven to 350°F (180°C). Blend first 6 ingredients together in mixing bowl until moistened. Beat at medium speed until smooth, about 2 minutes.

Sprinkle pecans evenly in bottom of ungreased 10 inch (25 cm) angel food tube pan. Pour batter carefully over top. Bake in oven until an inserted wooden pick comes out clean, about 50 to 60 minutes. Let stand 30 minutes. Loosen sides and center with knife. Turn out onto plate. Serve as is or with a spoonful of topping on each slice.

**RUM TOPPING**

| | | |
|---|---|---|
| Envelope of dessert topping mix | 1 | 1 |
| Instant chocolate pudding mix, 4 serving size | 1 | 1 |
| Rum, light or dark, to taste (or 1 1/2 tsp., 7 mL, rum flavoring, plus water) | 1/4 cup | 50 mL |
| Cold milk | 1 1/2 cups | 350 mL |
| Almonds, sliced or slivered (optional) | | |

Beat first 4 ingredients together in small deep bowl until fluffy, about 4 minutes. Serve over cake or use as frosting. Makes about 4 cups (1 L). May also be served over slices of angel food cake.

For an extra touch sprinkle with toasted sliced or slivered almonds.

# CHOCOLATE CARROT CAKE

*Cream cheese and carrots add moisture. The addition of spices adds to the chocolate flavor.*

| | | |
|---|---|---|
| Light chocolate cake mix, 2 layer size | 1 | 1 |
| Water | 1/2 cup | 125 mL |
| Eggs | 3 | 3 |
| Granulated sugar | 1/3 cup | 75 mL |
| Cream cheese, softened | 4 oz. | 125 g |
| Cinnamon | 1 tsp. | 5 mL |
| Nutmeg | 1/4 tsp. | 1 mL |
| Finely grated carrot | 2 cups | 450 mL |

Preheat oven to 350°F (180°C). Combine first 7 ingredients in mixing bowl. Beat slowly to moisten. Beat at medium speed until smooth, about 2 minutes.

Stir in carrot to distribute evenly. Scrape into greased 9 × 13 inch (22 × 33 cm) pan. Bake in oven until an inserted wooden pick comes out clean, about 40 to 50 minutes. Cool before frosting. Frost with Chocolate Cheese Icing, page 145.

# DEVIL'S POTATO CAKE

*Very light - certainly too light for the devil!*

| | | |
|---|---|---|
| Devil's Food cake mix, 2 layer size | 1 | 1 |
| Mashed potato | 1 cup | 250 mL |
| Butter or margarine, softened | 1/2 cup | 125 mL |
| Eggs | 3 | 3 |
| Water | 1/2 cup | 125 mL |
| Cinnamon | 1 tsp. | 5 mL |
| Nutmeg | 1/2 tsp. | 2 mL |
| Chopped walnuts | 1/2 cup | 125 mL |

Preheat oven to 350°F (180°C). Measure first 7 ingredients into mixing bowl. Beat until smooth.

Stir in walnuts. Turn into greased 10 inch (25 cm) angel food tube pan. Bake in oven for 40 to 50 minutes until an inserted wooden pick comes out clean. Let cool to lukewarm then remove from pan. Glaze with Chocolate Glaze, page 146.

*A yummy chocolate cake with a toffee and chocolate filling baked right in it.*

| | | |
|---|---|---|
| German chocolate cake mix, 2 layer size | 1 | 1 |
| Butter or margarine | 1 cup | 250 mL |
| Brown sugar, packed | 1 cup | 250 mL |
| Corn syrup | 1/4 cup | 60 mL |
| Sweetened condensed milk | 1 cup | 250 mL |
| Chopped pecans or walnuts | 1 cup | 250 mL |
| Semisweet chocolate chips | 1 cup | 250 mL |
| Chopped pecans or walnuts | 1 cup | 250 mL |

Preheat oven to 350°F (180°C). Prepare cake mix according to package directions. Divide mixture in half. Pour 1/2 into greased 9 × 13 inch (22 × 33 cm) pan. Set other 1/2 batter aside. Bake in oven for 15 minutes.

Meanwhile put butter, sugar, syrup and milk into heavy saucepan. Heat and stir until it boils. Boil 5 minutes stirring continually as it burns easily and quickly. Pour over baked cake.

Sprinkle with first amount of pecans and chips. Pour second 1/2 batter over top.

Sprinkle with remaining pecans. Bake for about 25 to 30 minutes more until an inserted wooden pick comes out clean.

**Variation:** For an alternate toffee filling to use to replace butter, brown sugar, corn syrup and sweetened condensed milk, combine 14 oz. (398 g) bag caramels, 1/2 cup (125 mL) evaporated milk, 3/4 cup (175 mL) butter in top of double boiler over boiling water. Heat to melt. Stir often. Spread over first layer as directed.

Pictured on page 17.

Paré Pointer

*Learn from fish. They are in no difficulty if they keep their mouths shut.*

# PISTACHIO CAKE

*This is a very pale green color. Delicate flavor.*

| | | |
|---|---|---|
| White cake mix, 2 layer size | 1 | 1 |
| Pistachlo instant pudding,<br>4 serving size | 1 | 1 |
| Water | 1 cup | 225 mL |
| Cooking oil | 1/2 cup | 125 mL |
| Eggs | 4 | 4 |
| Almond flavoring | 1/2 tsp. | 2 mL |

Preheat oven to 350°F (180°C). Combine all ingredients together in mixing bowl. Beat slowly to moisten. Beat at medium speed for 2 minutes. Bake in greased and floured 12 cup (2.7 L) bundt pan or a 10 inch (25 cm) angel food tube pan. Bake in oven for about 50 minutes. If using 9 × 13 inch (22 × 33 cm) pan bake for about 35 to 45 minutes until an inserted wooden pick comes out clean. Cool for 20 to 30 minutes. Turn out of pan. Before serving, sift icing (confectioner's) sugar over top or top with a vanilla glaze or frost with Pistachio Icing.

**PISTACHIO ICING**

| | | |
|---|---|---|
| Pistachio instant pudding,<br>4 serving size | 1 | 1 |
| Cold milk | 1 cup | 225 mL |
| Frozen whipped topping, thawed | 1 cup | 225 mL |

Mix all together. Add more topping if you want a larger amount of icing. Frost cake.

# CHOCOLATE ZUCCHINI CAKE

*Scrumptious. So moist and chocolaty.*

| | | |
|---|---|---|
| Chocolate cake mix, 2 layer size | 1 | 1 |
| Buttermilk or water | 1/2 cup | 125 mL |
| Cooking oil | 1/3 cup | 75 mL |
| Eggs | 3 | 3 |
| Cinnamon | 1/2 tsp. | 2 mL |
| Semisweet chocolate chips | 1 cup | 225 mL |
| Unpeeled and grated zucchini | 11/2 cups | 350 mL |

*(continued on next page)*

Preheat oven to 350°F (180°C). Slowly beat first 5 ingredients together in mixing bowl. Beat at medium speed until smooth, about 2 minutes.

Fold in chocolate chips and zucchini. Scrape into greased 9 × 13 inch (22 × 33 cm) pan. Bake in oven for about 35 to 40 minutes until an inserted wooden pick comes out clean. Cool and ice with Simple Chocolate Icing, page 148.

# ALMOST A SCRATCH CAKE

*Moist enough to seem home-made.*

| | | |
|---|---|---|
| Yellow cake mix, 2 layer size | 1 | 1 |
| Instant vanilla pudding mix, 4 serving size | 1 | 1 |
| Water | 1 cup | 225 mL |
| Cooking oil | 1/2 cup | 125 mL |
| Eggs | 4 | 4 |

Preheat oven to 350°F (180°C). Beat all ingredients together slowly in mixing bowl until moistened. Beat on medium speed for 2 minutes. Turn into greased and floured 12 cup (2.7 L) bundt pan. Bake in oven for 45 to 50 minutes until an inserted wooden pick comes out clean. Let stand in pan 20 minutes. Turn out onto rack or plate.

**MAPLE NUT CAKE:** Add 1 1/2 tsp. (7 mL) maple flavoring and 1/2 cup (125 mL) chopped pecans. Looks great. Tastes great.

**BANANA CAKE:** Use instant banana pudding mix instead of vanilla. Instead of just water, mash 1 banana and pack into measuring cup. Add water to make 1 cup (225 mL). This makes a tender, light cake that doesn't have the firmness of a banana loaf. Good flavor.

**CHOCOLATE POUND CAKE:** Use chocolate cake mix instead of yellow.

**SPICE CAKE:** Use spice cake mix instead of yellow.

**STRAWBERRY SHORTCAKE:** Bake white, yellow or chocolate cake mix in two 8 or 9 inch (20 or 22 cm) round layer pans. Fill and cover with sweetened mashed strawberries. Top with whipped cream.

**ORANGE CAKE:** Use orange cake mix. Use prepared orange juice instead of water.

**LEMON CAKE:** Use lemon cake mix and lemon pudding instead of yellow cake and vanilla pudding.

# CHOCOLATE PEANUT BUTTER CAKE

*Two flavor favorites together. Peanut butter taste is mild.*

| | | |
|---|---|---|
| Chocolate cake mix, 2 layer size | 1 | 1 |
| Smooth peanut butter | 1/2 cup | 125 mL |
| Eggs | 3 | 3 |
| Water | 1 1/4 cups | 300 mL |

Preheat oven to 350°F (180°C). Mix all ingredients slowly to moisten then beat 2 minutes until smooth. Divide between 2 greased round 8 or 9 inch (20 or 22 cm) round layer pans. Bake in oven until an inserted wooden pick comes out clean, about 30 minutes. Cool and frost with Peanut Butter Icing, page 141.

# CHOCOLATE RUM ICING

*Don't allow any tasting or you won't have enough left. Smooth as satin and absolutely yummy.*

| | | |
|---|---|---|
| Semisweet chocolate chips | 1 cup | 250 mL |
| Evaporated milk | 1/2 cup | 125 mL |
| Rum flavoring | 1 tsp. | 5 mL |

Melt chocolate chips in evaporated milk in small saucepan. Stir often. Remove from heat.

Stir in rum flavoring. Cool until spreadable. It will need to be quite cool. Makes 1 cup (250 mL).

# LEMON FILLING

*Smooth with just the right tang.*

| | | |
|---|---|---|
| Water | 3/4 cup | 175 mL |
| Lemon juice | 3 tbsp. | 50 mL |
| Grated lemon rind | 1 tsp. | 5 mL |
| Granulated sugar | 1/2 cup | 125 mL |
| Cornstarch | 2 tbsp. | 30 mL |
| Salt | 1/8 tsp. | 0.5 mL |
| Egg | 1 | 1 |

*(continued on next page)*

Put water, lemon juice and rind into saucepan over medium heat. Bring to a boil.

Meanwhile, mix sugar, cornstarch and salt together in small bowl. Add egg. Stir well. While stirring, add to boiling liquid until it boils and thickens. Cool. Makes about 1 1/3 cups (300 mL).

**ORANGE FILLING:** Omit water, lemon juice and lemon rind. Use 1 cup (225 mL) prepared orange juice and 1 tsp. (5 mL) grated orange rind.

# BURNT SUGAR SYRUP

*With this on hand you can make a burnt sugar cake with no extra fuss. Keeps indefinitely.*

| | | |
|---|---|---|
| **Granulated sugar** | **2 cups** | **500 mL** |
| **Water** | **1 cup** | **250 mL** |

Put sugar into large heavy frying pan over medium-low heat. Stir often as it melts. When it becomes a dark butterscotch color remove from heat.

Add about 1/4 of the water carefully. It will sputter furiously. Stir. Pour in the rest of the water. Return to medium heat. Stir until it dissolves. Color will now be a very dark brown. Cool before pouring into jar. Cover with lid and store in cupboard. Makes about 1 1/3 cups (325 mL).

# BANANA BUTTER ICING

*Give an extra banana boost to a banana cake or use on a peanut butter or white cake.*

| | | |
|---|---|---|
| **Butter or margarine, softened** | **1/4 cup** | **50 mL** |
| **Mashed banana** | **1/2 cup** | **125 mL** |
| **Lemon juice** | **1/2 tsp.** | **2 mL** |
| **Vanilla** | **1/2 tsp.** | **2 mL** |
| **Icing (confectioner's) sugar** | **3 1/4 cups** | **725 mL** |

Cream butter, banana, lemon juice and vanilla.

Slowly beat in icing sugar adding more if needed to make a nice fluffy, spreadable icing. Makes about 2 1/3 cups (525 mL).

# DATE FILLING

*Use to fill a two layer chocolate cake. Finish it off with a chocolate icing or Seven Minute Icing, page 147 or variation.*

| | | |
|---|---|---|
| Chopped dates | 1 cup | 250 mL |
| Granulated sugar | 1/4 cup | 60 mL |
| Water | 1/2 cup | 125 mL |
| Lemon juice | 1 tsp. | 5 mL |
| Vanilla | 1/2 tsp. | 2 mL |

Put dates, sugar, water and lemon juice in small saucepan. Simmer slowly. Stir often. Mixture should be thick and spreadable like jam.

Remove from heat and add vanilla. Stir well. Makes about 3/4 cup (200 mL).

# CARAMEL ICING

*The best flavor for all ages. Good on any cake. Good by the spoonful.*

| | | |
|---|---|---|
| Brown sugar, packed | 1/2 cup | 125 mL |
| Cream or milk | 3 tbsp. | 50 mL |
| Butter or margarine | 1/4 cup | 60 mL |
| Icing (confectioner's) sugar | 1 1/2 cups | 375 mL |

Heat brown sugar, cream and butter in medium saucepan until it boils. Boil for 2 minutes. Remove from heat. Cool.

Add icing sugar. Beat until smooth. Add more milk or icing sugar until of spreading consistency. Makes about 1 1/3 cups (325 mL).

Pictured on page 125.

# WHITE CHOCOLATE ICING

*This has a nice flavor. Try it with a white or chocolate cake as well as with a white chocolate cake.*

| | | |
|---|---|---|
| White baking chocolate squares | 4 × 1 oz. | 4 × 28 g |
| Butter or margarine | 1/4 cup | 60 mL |
| Vanilla | 1 tsp. | 5 mL |
| Milk | 2 tbsp. | 30 mL |
| Medium coconut | 1/2 cup | 125 mL |
| Chopped pecans or walnuts | 1/2 cup | 125 mL |
| Icing (confectioner's) sugar | 3/4 cup | 175 mL |

*(continued on next page)*

Put first 4 ingredients into saucepan over medium heat. Stir to melt. Remove from heat.

Add coconut, pecans and icing sugar. Add more sugar to thicken or more milk if needed to make proper spreading consistency. Fill and ice cake. Makes 1¹/₄ cups (275 mL).

# INSTANT PUDDING ICING

*A nice light soft icing.*

| | | |
|---|---|---|
| Envelope topping mix, such as Dream Whip | 1 | 1 |
| Instant pudding mix, 4 serving size | 1 | 1 |
| Milk | 1¹/₂ cups | 350 mL |
| Vanilla | ¹/₂ tsp. | 2 mL |

Combine all 4 ingredients in small mixing bowl. Mix to moisten. Beat about 5 minutes until mixture will stand in peaks. Makes about 4 cups (900 mL).

**Variation:** The lemon instant pudding mix is outstanding. Also the butter pecan. The vanilla is very versatile. Just try them all to decide your favorite.

# PINEAPPLE FILLING

*Soft and delicate.*

| | | |
|---|---|---|
| Crushed pineapple with juice | 14 oz. | 398 mL |
| Cornstarch | 3 tbsp. | 50 mL |
| Granulated sugar | ¹/₂ cup | 125 mL |
| Medium coconut | ¹/₂ cup | 125 mL |
| Lemon juice | 1 tsp. | 5 mL |
| Whipping cream (or 1 envelope topping) | 1 cup | 250 mL |
| Toasted coconut | 2 tbsp. | 30 mL |

Put first 5 ingredients into saucepan. Stir. Place over medium heat. Stir until it boils and thickens. Remove from heat. Chill.

Whip cream until stiff. Fold into chilled mixture. Spread between layers and frost cake or cover top layer.

Sprinkle with toasted coconut. Makes a generous 4 cups (900 mL).

# STRAWBERRY FLUFF

*This melts in your mouth instantly. It may remind you of cotton candy.*

| | | |
|---|---|---|
| Egg white | 1 | 1 |
| Granulated sugar | ½ cup | 225 mL |
| Frozen sliced strawberries with juice, thawed | ⅓ × 15 oz. | ⅓ × 425 g |
| Salt | ⅛ tsp. | 0.5 mL |

Put all 4 ingredients into top of double boiler. Beat with electric beater to mix well. Place over rapidly boiling water. Continue beating while it cooks until stiff peaks form when beater is lifted. Remove from heat and spread over cake. Makes about 4 cups (900 mL).

# BOILED CHOCOLATE ICING

*Like a fudge icing but this one doesn't require any beating. Simple and good.*

| | | |
|---|---|---|
| Brown sugar, packed | ½ cup | 125 mL |
| Water | ¼ cup | 60 mL |
| Butter or margarine | 3 tbsp. | 45 mL |
| Cocoa | 2 tbsp. | 30 mL |
| Icing (confectioner's) sugar | 1 cup | 250 mL |
| Vanilla | 1 tsp. | 5 mL |

Put first 4 ingredients into saucepan. Stir. Bring to a boil. Boil for 3 minutes. Remove from heat. Cool.

Add icing sugar and vanilla. Stir. Add a bit more icing sugar if needed. Makes about ¾ cup (200 mL).

# CREAMY FROSTING

*Very creamy. Very good. A white icing that looks like whipped cream.*

| | | |
|---|---|---|
| Milk | 1 cup | 225 mL |
| All-purpose flour | 2 tbsp. | 30 mL |
| Butter or margarine, softened | 1 cup | 250 mL |
| Granulated sugar | 1 cup | 250 mL |
| Vanilla | 1 tsp. | 5 mL |

*(continued on next page)*

Whisk milk into flour in small saucepan until smooth. Heat and stir until it boils and thickens. Cool thoroughly.

Cream butter, sugar and vanilla in bowl until light and fluffy. Add thickened milk. Beat until mixture resembles whipped cream. Makes enough to fill and frost 2 layer cake, about 3½ cups (825 mL).

# LEMON CHEESE FROSTING

*Exquisite flavor and so creamy.*

| | | |
|---|---|---|
| Cream cheese, softened | 8 oz. | 250 g |
| Butter or margarine | ¼ cup | 50 mL |
| Lemon juice | 2 tbsp. | 30 mL |
| Grated lemon rind | 2 tsp. | 10 mL |
| Vanilla | 1 tsp. | 5 mL |
| Icing (confectioner's) sugar | 5 cups | 1.1 L |

Beat cream cheese, butter, lemon juice, lemon rind and vanilla together until smooth and fluffy.

Add icing sugar in 2 additions. Beat until creamy. Add more icing sugar or juice as needed for easy spreading. Makes about 3⅔ cups (825 mL).

Pictured on page 89.

# PEANUT BUTTER ICING

*A mild delicate flavor. Scrumptious.*

| | | |
|---|---|---|
| Butter or margarine, softened | ¼ cup | 60 mL |
| Smooth peanut butter | ¼ cup | 60 mL |
| Vanilla | ½ tsp. | 2 mL |
| Salt | ⅛ tsp. | 0.5 mL |
| Icing (confectioner's) sugar | 2 cups | 500 mL |
| Milk | 3 tbsp. | 50 mL |

Combine all ingredients together in bowl. Beat until smooth. Makes about 1⅓ cups (300 mL).

**Variation:** Add ¼ tsp. (1 mL) cinnamon. Try this on a spice cake or apple cake.

Pictured on page 17.

# ORANGE FILLING AND FROSTING

*Soft and smooth and mouth-watering. Complements an orange cake but try it on a chocolate cake. Gorgeous.*

| | | |
|---|---|---|
| **Vanilla pudding powder (not instant), 4 serving size** | 1 | 1 |
| **Cornstarch** | 1 tsp. | 5 mL |
| **Frozen condensed orange juice, thawed** | 6 oz. | 170 g |
| **Water (use juice can to measure)** | 6 oz. | 170 g |
| **Whipping cream (or 1 envelope topping)** | 1 cup | 250 mL |
| **Toasted almonds (brown in 350°F, 180°C oven for 5 minutes or so, stirring often), or use orange sections or coconut** | 1/2 cup | 125 mL |

Stir pudding powder and cornstarch together in saucepan. Mix in orange juice and water. Heat and stir over medium heat until it boils and thickens. Chill thoroughly.

Whip cream until stiff. Fold into chilled pudding. Makes about 2$\frac{1}{2}$ cups (600 mL) filling or frosting, enough to fill and ice 2 layer cake.

Sprinkle toasted almonds over top.

1. Dark Chocolate Cake page 65 with Chocolate Cheese Icing page 145
2. Black Forest Cake page 74

# CREAM CHEESE ICING

*The only icing for carrot cakes but also good on any other kind of spice cake. Make half for one layer cake.*

| | | |
|---|---|---|
| Cream cheese, softened | 8 oz. | 250 g |
| Icing (confectioner's) sugar | 4 cups | 1 L |
| Butter or margarine, softened | 1/4 cup | 50 mL |
| Vanilla | 2 tsp. | 10 mL |

Put all ingredients into mixing bowl. Beat slowly at first to combine then beat at medium speed until light and fluffy. More or less icing sugar may be added as desired. Makes about 3 1/2 cups (800 mL).

Pictured on page 107 and 125.

**CHOCOLATE CHEESE ICING:** Beat in 1/2 cup (125 mL) cocoa or more if you wish. Add 1/2 tsp. (2 mL) of cinnamon for a surprisingly good flavor boost.

Pictured on page 107 and 143.

**CHEESE PECAN FROSTING:** Stir in 1 cup (225 mL) finely chopped pecans to Cream Cheese Icing.

**Note:** Less icing sugar may be added. The end result will be not as sweet and will be less quantity.

# CHOCOLATE PEANUT BUTTER FROSTING

*A perfect match for a chocolate peanut butter cake. Try it on a banana cake or even a white cake.*

| | | |
|---|---|---|
| Brown sugar, packed | 1/2 cup | 125 mL |
| Butter or margarine | 2 tbsp. | 30 mL |
| Light cream or milk | 1/4 cup | 60 mL |
| Smooth peanut butter | 1/2 cup | 125 mL |
| Cocoa | 3 tbsp. | 50 mL |
| Icing (confectioner's) sugar | 1 cup | 250 mL |
| Vanilla | 1/2 tsp. | 2 mL |

Put brown sugar, butter and cream into medium saucepan over medium heat. Stir. Bring to a boil. Boil 1 minute. Remove from heat.

Add remaining ingredients. Add more icing sugar or cream to obtain spreading consistency. Makes about 1 2/3 cups (400 mL).

**CHOCO PEANUT GLAZE:** Make only 1/2 recipe, omitting butter. Add cream to make desired consistency.

# VANILLA GLAZE

*In no time at all this is ready to give a thin coating or a drizzle over any cake, especially those made in tube pans.*

| Icing (confectioner's) sugar | 1 cup | 250 mL |
|---|---|---|
| Water | 1 tbsp. | 15 mL |
| Vanilla | 1/4 tsp. | 1 mL |

Mix all ingredients together well. Add more icing sugar or water to make proper consistency for a barely pourable glaze.

Pictured on page 125.

**LEMON GLAZE:** Omit water and vanilla. Add same amount of lemon juice.

**ORANGE GLAZE:** Omit water and vanilla. Add same amount of frozen condensed orange juice.

**BROWN ORANGE GLAZE:** Make Orange Glaze using brown sugar instead of icing sugar.

**RUM GLAZE:** Add 1/2 tsp. (2 mL) rum flavoring instead of vanilla.

**CHOCOLATE GLAZE:** Add 2 tbsp. (30 mL) cocoa or more if you want it darker. More water will be needed.

**CHERRY GLAZE:** Omit water and vanilla. Add same amount of maraschino cherry juice as water. Add 1/4 tsp. (1 mL) almond flavoring.

**MARBLE GLAZE:** Glaze cake with Vanilla Glaze. Let dry. Spoon Chocolate Glaze over top being sure some of the white is still showing. Especially nice on a marble cake.

**CHOCOLATE RUM GLAZE:** Add 1/2 tsp. (2 mL) rum flavoring to Chocolate Glaze.

**CHOCOLATE DRIZZLE:** Melt some semisweet chocolate baking squares or chips over hot water. Drizzle around top outside edges letting it run down sides or drizzle over top of cake.

**BROWN SUGAR GLAZE:** Add 1/2 cup (125 mL) brown sugar and an additional 1 tsp. (15 mL) water.

# SEVEN MINUTE FROSTING

*A shiny soft white icing that resembles half melted marshmallows. It swirls prettlly.*

| | | |
|---|---|---|
| **Egg whites** | 2 | 2 |
| **Granulated sugar** | 1¹/₂ cups | 350 mL |
| **Cold water** | ¹/₃ cup | 75 mL |
| **Light corn syrup** | 1¹/₂ tsp. | 7 mL |
| **Vanilla** | 1 tsp. | 5 mL |

Put egg whites, sugar, water and syrup in top of double boiler. Beat until mixed well. Place over rapidly boiling water. Beat constantly with electric beater while it cooks for 7 minutes or until it will stand in peaks when beater is raised. Remove from heat.

Add vanilla. Beat. Fills and frosts 2 layer cake, 8 or 9 inch (20 or 22 cm).

**SEAFOAM FROSTING:** Omit granulated sugar. Add 1¹/₂ cups (375 mL) brown sugar and 1 tsp. (5 mL) maple flavoring. Very light butterscotch color. Extra flavorful. Children love this icing. A poppy seed chiffon is extra good encased in this.

**MOCHA FLUFF:** Add 1 tsp. (5 mL) instant coffee granules, crushed, or more to taste. Similar in color to Seafoam Frosting with a mild coffee flavor. Just the right finishing touch.

**CHERRY FLUFF:** Add only 3 tbsp. (50 mL) water, 3 tbsp. (50 mL) maraschino cherry juice and ¹/₈ tsp (0.5 mL) almond flavoring. A wee bit of red food coloring can be added for color at the last. Not only pretty but tasty as well. This pink icing is really showy.

**MARSHMALLOW ICING:** Add 1 cup (250 mL) tiny marshmallows at the last. Beat until they melt. This may be used to fill a jelly roll as well.

*Try facing the music with your nose to the grindstone and your back to the wall.*

# SIMPLE CHOCOLATE ICING

*This good quick icing is one of the most used. Always acceptable and often preferred.*

| Icing (confectioner's) sugar | 2¹/₂ cups | 625 mL |
|---|---|---|
| Cocoa | ¹/₂ cup | 125 mL |
| Butter or margarine, softened | 6 tbsp. | 100 mL |
| Milk or water | ¹/₄ cup | 60 mL |
| Vanilla | 1 tsp. | 5 mL |

Measure all ingredients into mixing bowl. Beat slowly until all moistened. Add more milk or icing sugar if needed. Beat until smooth and light. Fill and ice 2 layer cake. Makes about 2 cups (500 mL).

**Note:** By varying the amount of cocoa added this will make several shades from light to dark.

**Variation:** Prepared coffee may be added instead of milk or water. An egg yolk may be stirred in if desired.

Pictured on page 125.

**CHOCOLATE MINT ICING:** Stir in some mint flavoring, about ¹/₂ tsp. (2 mL). Add more to taste for a more minty flavor.

**CHOCOLATE MOCHA ICING:** Use prepared coffee instead of milk or water.

Pictured on page 89.

# SNOW WHITE ICING

*This is the whitest of the whites. Great for piping onto cakes. Tints easily for truer colors.*

| Icing (confectioner's) sugar | 3 cups | 700 mL |
|---|---|---|
| Milk | 3 tbsp. | 50 mL |
| Shortening, such as Crisco, softened | ³/₄ cup | 175 mL |
| Vanilla | ¹/₂ tsp. | 2 mL |
| Almond flavoring | ¹/₂ tsp. | 2 mL |
| Salt | ¹/₄ tsp. | 1 mL |

Put all ingredients into small mixing bowl. Beat together well. Add more milk or icing sugar if needed for easy spreading. Makes about 3 cups (700 mL).

*Assorted fillings for many different cakes. For more filling simply double the recipe.*

| | | |
|---|---|---|
| **Milk** | **1 cup** | **225 mL** |
| **Granulated sugar** | **$1/3$ cup** | **75 mL** |
| **All-purpose flour** | **3 tbsp.** | **50 mL** |
| **Salt** | **$1/8$ tsp.** | **0.5 mL** |
| **Egg** | **1** | **1** |
| **Vanilla** | **$1/2$ tsp.** | **2 mL** |

Heat milk in small heavy saucepan over medium heat until it boils.

Meanwhile mix sugar, flour and salt together. Mix in egg. Stir into boiling milk until it returns to a boil and thickens.

Remove from heat. Add vanilla. Cool. This will curdle if boiled too long. If you would rather, cook it in double boiler. Makes $1^1/3$ cups (300 mL).

**COCONUT CREAM FILLING:** Add $1/3$ cup (75 mL) medium coconut.

**BANANA CREAM FILLING:** Add $1/2$ cup (125 mL) mashed banana. Best served the same day.

**ALMOND CREAM FILLING:** Omit vanilla. Add $1/4$ tsp. (1 mL) almond flavoring and about $1/4$ cup (60 mL) finely chopped toasted almonds.

**MOCHA CREAM FILLING:** Add $1^1/2$ tsp. (7 mL) instant coffee granules.

**PINEAPPLE CREAM FILLING:** Omit vanilla. Add $1/2$ cup (125 mL) crushed pineapple, well drained and 1 tsp. (5 mL) lemon juice.

**CHOCOLATE CREAM FILLING:** Reduce milk to $2/3$ cup (150 mL). Add 2 × 1 oz. (2 × 28 g) unsweetened baking chocolate squares, cut into small pieces, to hot filling. Stir to melt.

**CARAMEL CREAM FILLING:** Use brown sugar instead of granulated sugar. Reduce milk to $3/4$ cup (150 mL). Add $1/4$ cup (50 mL) Burnt Sugar Syrup, page 137.

*Monsters have their favorite flowers — mari-ghouls and mourning gorys.*

# BUTTER ICING

*Quick and easy, one of these is bound to save the day.*

| Icing (confectioner's) sugar | 2 cups | 500 mL |
|---|---|---|
| Butter or margarine, softened | ¼ cup | 60 mL |
| Cream, milk or water | 3 tbsp. | 45 mL |
| Vanilla | 1 tsp. | 5 mL |

Beat all ingredients together in bowl until smooth. Add more liquid or icing sugar as needed. Makes about 1⅓ cups (325 mL).

**CHERRY ICING:** Omit cream and vanilla. Add 3 tbsp. (45 mL) maraschino cherry juice. If you don't have any cherry juice use water plus a bit of red food coloring and ¼ tsp. (1 mL) cherry or almond flavoring.

**ORANGE ICING:** Omit cream and vanilla. Add frozen concentrated orange juice to moisten.

**COFFEE ICING:** Instead of cream add strong hot coffee.

Pictured on cover.

**MAPLE ICING:** Add ½ tsp. (2 mL) maple flavoring. Stir and taste adding more as desired.

**BURNT SUGAR ICING:** Use 2 tbsp. (30 mL) Burnt Sugar Syrup, page 137, as part of the liquid.

**PINK BUTTER ICING:** Add red food coloring to tint a pretty pink.

**GREEN BUTTER ICING:** Add green food coloring to tint a pale green.

Pictured on page 17.

# LEMON ICING

*Quick and easy. A superb icing.*

| Butter or margarine, softened | ½ cup | 125 mL |
|---|---|---|
| Lemon juice | 2 tbsp. | 30 mL |
| Vanilla | ½ tsp. | 2 mL |
| Icing (confectioner's) sugar | 3 cups | 675 mL |

Measure all ingredients into mixing bowl. Beat until fluffy. Add more icing sugar or juice for easy spreading. If lemon flavor is quite strong add water if more liquid is needed. Makes about 2 cups (450 mL).

Pictured on page 17.

# ■ METRIC CONVERSION ■

Throughout this book measurements are given in Imperial and Metric measure. To compensate for differences between the two measurements due to rounding, a full metric measure is not always used.

The cup used is the standard 8 fluid ounce. Temperature is given in degrees Fahrenheit and Celsius. Baking Pan measurements are in inches and centimetres as well as quarts and litres. An exact conversion is given below as well as the working equivalent (Standard Measure).

| IMPERIAL | METRIC | |
|---|---|---|
| | Exact Conversion | Standard Measure |
| **Spoons** | millilitre (mL) | millilitre (mL) |
| 1/4 teaspoon (tsp.) | 1.2 mL | 1 mL |
| 1/2 teaspoon (tsp.) | 2.4 mL | 2 mL |
| 1 teaspoon (tsp.) | 4.7 mL | 5 mL |
| 2 teaspoons (tsp.) | 9.4 mL | 10 mL |
| 1 tablespoon (tbsp.) | 14.2 mL | 15 mL |
| | | |
| **Cups** | | |
| 1/4 cup (4 tbsp.) | 56.8 mL | 50 mL |
| 1/3 cup (5 1/3 tbsp.) | 75.6 mL | 75 mL |
| 1/2 cup (8 tbsp.) | 113.7 mL | 125 mL |
| 2/3 cup (10 2/3 tbsp.) | 151.2 mL | 150 mL |
| 3/4 cup (12 tbsp.) | 170.5 mL | 175 mL |
| 1 cup (16 tbsp.) | 227.3 mL | 250 mL |
| 4 1/2 cups | 984.8 mL | 1000 mL, 1 litre (1 L) |
| | | |
| **Ounces (oz.)** | **Grams (g)** | **Grams (g)** |
| 1 oz. | 28.3 g | 30 g |
| 2 oz. | 56.7 g | 55 g |
| 3 oz. | 85.0 g | 85 g |
| 4 oz. | 113.4 g | 125 g |
| 5 oz. | 141.7 g | 140 g |
| 6 oz. | 170.1 g | 170 g |
| 7 oz. | 198.4 g | 200 g |
| 8 oz. | 226.8 g | 250 g |
| 16 oz. | 453.6 g | 500 g |
| 32 oz. | 917.2 g | 1000 g, 1 kilogram (1 kg) |

## OVEN TEMPERATURES

| Fahrenheit (°F) | Celsius (°C) |
|---|---|
| 175° | 80° |
| 200° | 100° |
| 225° | 110° |
| 250° | 120° |
| 275° | 140° |
| 300° | 150° |
| 325° | 160° |
| 350° | 180° |
| 375° | 190° |
| 400° | 200° |
| 425° | 220° |
| 450° | 230° |
| 475° | 240° |
| 500° | 260° |

## PANS, CASSEROLES

| Imperial | Metric | Imperial | Metric |
|---|---|---|---|
| 8x8 inch | 20x20 cm | 1 2/3 qt. | 2 L |
| 9x9 inch | 22x22 cm | 2 qt.. | 2.5 L |
| 9x13 inch | 22x33 cm | 3 1/3 qt. | 4 L |
| 10x15 inch | 25x38 cm | 1 qt. | 1.2 L |
| 11x17 inch | 28x43 cm | 1 1/4 qt. | 1.5 L |
| 8x2 inch round | 20x5 cm | 1 2/3 qt. | 2 L |
| 9x2 inch round | 22x5 cm | 2 qt. | 2.5 L |
| 10x4 1/2 inch tube | 25x11 cm | 4 1/4 qt. | 5 L |
| 8x4x3 inch loaf | 20x10x7 cm | 1 1/4 qt. | 1.5 L |
| 9x5x3 inch loaf | 23x12x7 cm | 1 2/3 qt. | 2 L |

# INDEX

## CAKE CUTTING PATTERNS

8 or 9 inch (20 or 22 cm) 36 pieces

8 or 9 inch (20 or 22 cm) 36 pieces

8 x 8 (20 x 20 cm) 32 pieces

  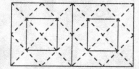

First cut 8 x 16 inch (20 x 32.5 cm)

Second cut

Third Cut 32 pieces

8 or 9 inch (20 or 22 cm)

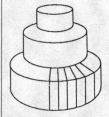   

Cut a vertical path around edge of second layer. Slice into wedges.

Cut a vertical path around edge of top layer. Slice into wedges.

Cut vertical path around edge of second layer. Slice into wedges.

Save top layer for an anniversary. Cut up other two layers if needed.

# Company's Coming cookbooks are available at retail locations throughout Canada!

## EXCLUSIVE mail order offer on next page

Buy any 2 cookbooks—choose a 3rd FREE of equal or less value than the lowest price paid.

### Original Series · CA$14.99 Canada · US$10.99 USA & International

| CODE | | CODE | | CODE | |
|------|----------------------|------|-----------------------|------|------------------|
| SQ | 150 Delicious Squares | KC | Kids Cooking | FD | Fondues |
| CA | Casseroles | CT | Cooking For Two | CCBE | The Beef Book |
| MU | Muffins & More | BB | Breakfasts & Brunches | ASI | Asian Cooking |
| SA | Salads | SC | Slow Cooker Recipes | CB | The Cheese Book |
| AP | Appetizers | ODM | One-Dish Meals | RC | The Rookie Cook |
| DE | Desserts | ST | Starters | RHR | Rush-Hour Recipes |
| SS | Soups & Sandwiches | SF | Stir-Fry | SW | Sweet Cravings |
| CO | Cookies | MAM | Make-Ahead Meals | YRG | Year-Round Grilling |
| PA | Pasta | PB | The Potato Book | GG | Garden Greens |
| BA | Barbecues | CCLFC | Low-Fat Cooking | CHC | Chinese Cooking |
| LR | Light Recipes | CCLFP | Low-Fat Pasta | PK | The Pork Book |
| PR | Preserves | CFK | Cook For Kids | | |
| CH | Chicken, Etc. | SCH | Stews, Chilies & Chowders | | |

### Greatest Hits Series

| CODE | CA$12.99 Canada  US$9.99 USA & International |
|------|----------------------------------------------|
| ITAL | Italian |
| MEX | Mexican |

### Lifestyle Series

| CODE | CA$16.99 Canada  US$12.99 USA & International |
|------|-----------------------------------------------|
| GR | Grilling |
| DC | Diabetic Cooking |

| CODE | CA$19.99 Canada  US$15.99 USA & International |
|------|-----------------------------------------------|
| HC | Heart-Friendly Cooking |

### Special Occasion Series

| CODE | CA$19.99 Canada  US$17.99 USA & International |
|------|-----------------------------------------------|
| GFK | Gifts from the Kitchen |
| CFS | Cooking for the Seasons |

| CODE | CA$22.99 Canada  US$17.99 USA & International |
|------|-----------------------------------------------|
| WC | Weekend Cooking |

| CODE | CA$24.99 Canada  US$19.99 USA & International |
|------|-----------------------------------------------|
| HFH | Home for the Holidays |
| DD | Decadent Desserts **NEW** Oct 1/03 |

Company's Coming COOKBOOKS®

COMPANY'S COMING PUBLISHING LIMITED
2311 – 96 Street
Edmonton, Alberta, Canada  T6N 1G3
Tel: (780) 450-6223  Fax: (780) 450-1857
www.companyscoming.com

# EXCLUSIVE Mail Order Offer
## See previous page for list of cookbooks

## Buy 2 Get 1 FREE!
Buy any 2 cookbooks—choose a **3rd FREE** of equal or less value than the lowest price paid.

| Quantity | Code | Title | Price Each | Price Total |
|---|---|---|---|---|
| | | | $ | $ |
| | | | | |
| | | | | |
| | | | | |
| | | | | |
| | | | | |

DON'T FORGET
to indicate your
FREE BOOK(S).
(see exclusive mail order
offer above)
please print

| | | | |
|---|---|---|---|
| | TOTAL BOOKS (including FREE) | TOTAL BOOKS PURCHASED: | $ |

|  | International | Canada & USA |
|---|---|---|
| Plus Shipping & Handling (per destination) | $7.00 (one book) | $5.00 (1-3 books) |
| Additional Books (including FREE books) | $ ($2.00 each) | $ ($1.00 each) |
| Sub-Total | $ | $ |
| Canadian residents add G.S.T(7%) | | $ |
| **TOTAL AMOUNT ENCLOSED** | $ | $ |

## The Fine Print

- Orders outside Canada must be **PAID IN US FUNDS** by cheque or money order drawn on Canadian or US bank or by credit card.
- Make cheque or money order payable to: **COMPANY'S COMING PUBLISHING LIMITED.**
- Prices are expressed in Canadian dollars for Canada, US dollars for USA & International and are subject to change without prior notice.
- Orders are shipped surface mail. For courier rates, visit our web-site: **companyscoming.com** or contact us:
  Tel: (780) 450-6223 Fax: (780) 450-1857.
- Sorry, no C.O.D's.

## Gift Giving

- Let us help you with your gift giving!
- We will send cookbooks directly to the recipients of your choice if you give us their names and addresses.
- Please specify the titles you wish to send to each person.
- If you would like to include your personal note or card, we will be pleased to enclose it with your gift order.

☐ MasterCard    ☐ VISA _____
Expiry date

Account # _____

Name of cardholder _____

Cardholder's signature _____

## Shipping Address
### Send the cookbooks listed above to:

Name: _____

Street: _____

City: _____ Prov./State: _____

Country: _____ Postal Code/Zip: _____

Tel: ( ) _____

E-mail address: _____

☐ YES! Please send a catalogue _____

# New October 1st, 2003

There's a magical force at work—one that can't possibly be ignored. It can mystically transform the ordinary into the extraordinary, turn frowns into smiles and halt a dinner conversation in its tracks. Welcome to the enchanting world of *Decadent Desserts!*

Enter in and allow yourself to be engulfed by a sweet feast of stunning desserts. Luscious colour photographs inspire and tantalize, showcasing every lovingly tested recipe. Dare to explore your hidden gourmet talents. Let the informative "how-to" guides and illustrated step-by-step instructions chart your course. Become renowned for creating your own trademark dessert garnishes and decorations.

Charm family and friends with something wonderfully delectable, sinfully sweet, incredibly rich. Add a little magic to your next dinner—cast your spell with *Decadent Desserts!*

# Complete your Original Series Collection!

- ❏ 150 Delicious Squares
- ❏ Casseroles
- ❏ Muffins & More
- ❏ Salads
- ❏ Appetizers
- ❏ Desserts
- ❏ Soups & Sandwiches
- ❏ Cookies
- ❏ Pasta
- ❏ Barbecues
- ❏ Light Recipes
- ❏ Preserves
- ❏ Chicken, Etc.
- ❏ Kids Cooking
- ❏ Cooking For Two
- ❏ Breakfasts & Brunches
- ❏ Slow Cooker Recipes
- ❏ One-Dish Meals
- ❏ Starters
- ❏ Stir-Fry
- ❏ Make-Ahead Meals
- ❏ The Potato Book
- ❏ Low-Fat Cooking
- ❏ Low-Fat Pasta
- ❏ Cook For Kids
- ❏ Stews, Chilies & Chowders
- ❏ Fondues
- ❏ The Beef Book
- ❏ Asian Cooking
- ❏ The Cheese Book
- ❏ The Rookie Cook
- ❏ Rush-Hour Recipes
- ❏ Sweet Cravings
- ❏ Year-Round Grilling
- ❏ Garden Greens
- ❏ Chinese Cooking
- ❏ The Pork Book

# COLLECT ALL Company's Coming Series Cookbooks!

## Greatest Hits Series
- ❏ Italian
- ❏ Mexican

## Special Occasion Series
- ❏ Gifts from the Kitchen
- ❏ Cooking for the Seasons
- ❏ Home for the Holidays
- ❏ Weekend Cooking
- ❏ Decadent Desserts  **NEW** Oct 1/03

## Lifestyle Series
- ❏ Grilling
- ❏ Diabetic Cooking
- ❏ Heart-Friendly Cooking

# Canada's most popular cookbooks!